W9-DJD-281

Landscapes of
SORRENTO, AMALFI *and* CAPRI

a countryside guide
Fifth edition

Julian Tippett

SUNFLOWER BOOKS

Fifth edition © 2008
Sunflower Books™
PO Box 36160
London SW7 3WS, UK
www.sunflowerbooks.co.uk

Published in the USA by
Hunter Publishing Inc
130 Campus Drive
Edison, NJ 08818
www.hunterpublishing.com

All rights reserved. No part
of this publication may be
reproduced, stored in a retrieval
system, or transmitted by any
form or by any means,
electronic, mechanical,
photocopying, recording or
otherwise, without the prior
written permission of the
publishers.

ISBN 978-1-85691-357-7

San Domenico (Walk segment 29)

Important note to the reader

We have tried to ensure that the descriptions and maps in this book are error-free at press date. The book will be updated, where necessary, whenever future printings permit. It will be very helpful for us to receive your comments (sent in care of the publishers, please) for the updating of future printings. Reports are also welcomed of the more remote walks successfully completed.

We also rely on those who use this book — especially walkers — to take along a good supply of common sense when they explore. If the route is not as we outline it here, and your way ahead is not secure, return to the point of departure. ***Never attempt to complete a tour or walk under hazardous conditions!*** Please read carefully the notes on pages 15 to 19, the Country code on page 136, and the introductory comments at the beginning of each walk segment. Explore *safely*, while at the same time respecting the beauty of the countryside.

This book differs slightly from other titles in the Landscapes Series. Originally published privately by the author as 'Walks from Amalfi', the book was so well received that we have preserved the original format of walk *segments and planners*, while at the same time expanding the area covered and adding car tours and excursions.

*With thanks to my wife, Pat, and to Antonio Calvano,
  for their encouragement*

Cover: view over Positano from the Sentiero degli Dei (Walk segment 26)
Title page: Villa Cimbrone, Ravello (Excursion 4, Walk segment 3)

Photographs and maps by the author
Sunflower Books and 'Landscapes' are Registered Trademarks.
A CIP catalogue record for this book is available from the British Library.
Printed and bound in China by WKT Company Ltd

⚘ Contents

Preface   4
Introduction   6
  The Amalfi Peninsula   7
  Planning a holiday   8
  Getting about   8
  Pronunciation guide   11
  The inner man   11
  Flora and fauna   12
  The footpaths — their nature and origin   14
  Hints to walkers   15
  The walk planners   17
  Guides and maps   18
Excursions with picnic   20
Touring   24
  Tour 1: CIRCUIT FROM SORRENTO   26
  Tour 2: SANTA MARIA DEL CASTELLO AND
      MONTE FAITO   28
  Tour 3: MONTE PERTUSO AND NOCELLE   29
  Tour 4: THE AGEROLA PLAIN   30
  MAJOR SIGHTS OUTSIDE THE REGION   30
  Tour 5: POGEROLA   32
  Tour 6: PONTONE   32
  Tour 7: TRAMONTI   33
Amalfi/Ravello (Walk segments 1-17)   34
  Plans of Amalfi and Ravello   36
  Walk segments and planner   39
Positano/Praiano (Walk segments 18-33)   58
  Plan of Positano   59
  Walk segments and planner   61
Conca dei Marini (Walk segments 34-38)   81
  Walk segments and planner   82
Maiori/Minori (Walk segments 39-46)   88
  Walk segments and planner   89
Sorrento (Walk segments 47-65)   100
  Plan of Sorrento   101
  Walk segments and planner   102
Capri (Walk segments 66-72)   121
  Walk segments and planner   122
Bus timetables   129
Useful web sites   133
Index   134
Country code for walkers and motorists   136
Fold-out area map   *inside back cover*

❀ Preface

The coastal towns south of Naples have attracted travellers for a hundred years and more, Wagner, Ibsen, Ruskin and Longfellow being amongst the more famous. Today visitors come in their thousands to stay in Sorrento or in small towns further along the coast, from where they visit Pompei, take a trip up Vesuvius or catch the ferry to Capri. They also come to soak up the sensational coastal scenery of soaring limestone cliffs, serpentine roads and clinging hillside villages. And they will spend time looking around the towns, drinking cappuccino in the bar of a small piazza, and perhaps relaxing by the pool. All the ingredients are in place for a leisurely Mediterranean holiday.

But if you like to walk, another ingredient will intrigue and tempt you. Accident of history and steepness of terrain have preserved a network of ancient footpaths which reaches from the towns into the surrounding countryside. These paths let you leave the bustle of town life and the clamour of motor traffic, to walk among lemon groves, visit hillside villages, see remote monasteries and, along the way, be regaled by the most stunning of views. The paths are often paved in stone or, if climbing the steep hillsides, consist of flights of steps. And the flowers are a constant delight: from broom and rosemary in March to freesias and cistus in May. In autumn, the woods are carpeted with cyclamen. Given a little effort, a whole new world awaits you.

Most of the paths described here can be followed easily by people who do not claim to be regular walkers, though committed hikers will like them just the same. The walks are described in such a way as to give many choices when planning an outing; where to go, how long, how energetic. Besides being flexible, the path network is splendidly accessible. Often you can start walking directly from the door of your hotel or, at most, a short bus journey is needed to reach the start of the walk. Just a few of the walks are for experts only, as you will see in the text.

4

When you are ready to explore the area in depth, but perhaps not wanting to walk too much, try one of the 'Excursions with picnic' suggested on pages 20-23; these are easy but attractive outings, ideal for hot or 'lazy' days. Or, if you are hiring a car, dip into the Touring section to get off the beaten track.

A great beauty of walking when abroad is that you get away from tourist haunts. Instead of meeting only people who are there for visitors, you come across farmers or others going about their daily lives. We (my wife and I) have met a craftsman intent on showing us his baskets made from split chestnut; a retired hotel porter who wanted to share a bottle of surprisingly good home-made wine; a farmer harvesting grapes who insisted on replacing the shop-bought grapes we were eating on our picnic. And you come across other like-minded walkers with a sense of adventure. Meeting people one-to-one on a footpath, you tend to get into conversation or, if your language skills are not up to it, there is at least mutual recognition, and especially so here where the local people are so friendly and open. In short, you feel included in the life of the countryside. This splendid feeling, together with the marvellous sights all around, make for an unbeatable combination. I hope the foregoing is persuasive enough to tempt you into trying some of these walks, but beware, you may become hooked!

On the flower-filled descent to the Torre Damecuta, with Ischia beyond (Walk segment 71 on Capri)

Introduction

The guide has been designed as a reference book to dip into according to need. This first section deals with topics that apply to the whole region — defining and describing the region covered by the guide, local transport, food and drink, how to plan a holiday here, advice on walking the paths, notes on flora and fauna. It is followed by a short section, 'Excursions with picnic', to give ideas for some outings based on *bus travel* which will take you off the beaten track with a minimum of physical effort. These trips often follow sections (usually downhill) of the main walks. Another short section, 'Touring', offers similar ideas for excursions for *motorists*.

The major part of the book is devoted to *walks* from the six main tourist areas. Certainly one, but perhaps two or three of these areas will be of interest to you — depending on where you are staying and whether you wish sometimes to take a bus or a boat to walk outside your 'home' territory

The walks are not described as separate complete routes as is usual in *Landscapes* guides, but as *segments,* each of which is a connecting link in the path network. You make up your own routes by stringing segments together to build a walk of the desired length and difficulty; to help you, there is a 'walk planner' diagram for each of the six areas. Once on the walk, detailed instructions enable you to follow each of the segments.

This arrangement gives great flexibility for planning walks to suit every need and is possible only because the footpaths here happen to form a true network, *but it does require some attention to learn the rules*. The detail of how to plan a walk is described on page 17. To get the most out of this book, you are urged to examine this explanation closely.

Preceding the walks in each of the six areas local information is given, such as a description of the terrain and any special transport arrangements. Town plans are included here, as well as a brief summary of the popular tourist sights. In general, however, this guide leaves the task of describing towns and historical sites to the many other publications so easily obtained near your hotel.

The Amalfi Peninsula

Sometimes also called the Sorrento Peninsula, this mountainous tongue of land forms the southern arm of the Bay of Naples, with Sorrento itself sitting near its tip on a shelf some 60 metres (200 feet) above the sea. The Lattari (derived from the Latin word for milk) mountains in the spine of the peninsula rise to 1440 metres (nearly 5000 feet), often presenting a majestic scene of great limestone cliffs and profound chasms. The world-famous Amalfi Coast occupies the southern edge of the peninsula and here lies that noted string of holiday resorts — Positano, Praiano, Amalfi, Minori and Maiori. All along the coastline the mountains rise steeply from the sea to make the tortuous road which connects the towns into the most exhilarating drive imaginable.

Of the famous towns of the region, the only one not located on the coast is Ravello, which sits in all its glory some 360 metres (1200 feet) high on an arm projecting south from the mountains, towering over the coastline nearby. Two high plains relieve the mountainous scene, Agerola and Tramonti, but otherwise the countryside is always either hilly or mountainous, perhaps being least steep behind Sorrento. Six kilometres off the tip of the peninsula lies the rocky island of Capri.

Looking west from the cemetery in Amalfi beyond the town to the hillside visited on Walk segment 9 and to Conca dei Marini on the skyline.

Excursion 4 and Walk segment 3: typical cast-iron lampposts frame the view east along the coast from the small piazza by Santa Maria Maddalena in Atrani (left), and belvedere at the Villa Cimbrone, Ravello.

Planning a holiday

Probably the easiest method of installing yourself in the region for a holiday, and possibly the cheapest, is to take a package tour which provides travel, transfers and hotel. With such a package and this book, you have a fine self-made walking or touring holiday. Check the location of the hotel in case it is some way out of town and would therefore entail a journey to get into the walking network.

For the independent traveller, all towns have a selection of hotels and pensions. Useful web sites are listed on page 133.

Getting about

The notes below outline the basic principles of using buses, trains and boats *in the region,* and show you how to transfer independently to your resort. Details of *local* transport are to be found in the area descriptions starting on page 34; bus timetables begin on page 129.

Bus services. The SITA company runs the out of town buses reliably and punctually, the odd strike *(sciopero)* excepted. The drivers are much to be admired for their patient, calm and skilled driving, often when faced with great congestion on the tortuous and narrow coastal corniche road. Services are relatively frequent.

Bus stops carry the legend FERMATA SITA. If you are taking a walk or going on one of the suggested outings, the name for the bus stop where you alight is given in the text (unless it is simply the name of the village). If you are uncertain of knowing when you have reached your stop, ask the driver to drop you off using this phrase: *'Per favore, ci può far scendere alla fermata ...*

Moody evening view of Capri and the Faraglione islands, seen from Termini (Excursion 13; Tour 1, Walk segments 52, 53, 58, 61 and 62)

(name of the stop)'. You could even write this out to show him; *'ci'* means 'us'; if travelling alone use *'mi'*.

Except for the local buses in Positano and Capri, tickets must be bought in advance at a local shop (typically a bar or tobacconist) or a SITA office. You validate the ticket on boarding the bus by offering it into the machine which stamps it and clips a corner. Do not expect the inspector to be sympathetic just because you are a visitor if you do not have a properly validated ticket. Since the tickets do not carry any destination, only a price, always think about buying the ticket for the return journey when getting your outbound tickets. If you are staying somewhere for more than a few days, it pays to keep a stock of tickets of the denominations you commonly use, in case you find yourself wanting to travel from a location where (or at a time when) tickets are unavailable. The fare structure is described on page 133.

Timetables are displayed in various locations, as described in the 'Getting about' section for each of the local areas (starting on page 34). Free copies of up-to-date timetables are available from the Sorrento tourist office and the Amalfi SITA ticket office. When reading timetables: *Giornale* = daily; *Feriale* = Mon-Sat; *Festivo* = Sundays and official holidays. You can download SITA timetables from the web at www.sitabus.it. Choose *linee regionali > Campania > orari*. Look for quadri vii, viii, xiii, xiv, and xv.

Trains. Both Naples and Salerno lie on the main west coast line, but trains are too infrequent to be of interest when travelling between the two cities. Better by bus.

Of much greater interest is the 'Circumvesuviana', a local narrow-gauge network. Frequent trains depart from the station alongside the main railway station in the Piazza Garibaldi in Naples to Sorrento (journey time about 1 hour). The trains on this line also stop at Pompei and Ercolano (Herculaneum).

Boats. All-year ferries *(traghetti)* and jet boats run between Naples, Sorrento and Capri. Summer-only services operate between Salerno, Amalfi, Positano, Capri and Sorrento. Timetables and fares leaflets can be picked up at quayside ticket kiosks. Also see various web sites (page 133).

How to get to your resort
Stage 1: from the airport to Naples
Independent travellers not having transfers arranged for them need first of all to reach Naples: either the Circumvesuviana station (below and beside Central station) for the train to **Sorrento***, or the SITA bus station for **Amalfi** and **Salerno**. The half-hourly airport bus ('Alibus' — tickets on board €3.00) will take you first to the stations and then to its terminus in Piazza Municipale. Here cross the road to the harbour side and turn left. After 400m/yds, by the first set of traffic lights, turn right into the SITA bus station on Molo Immacolatella.

For the return journey take the airport bus from near Central Station in Piazza Garibaldi (where the SITA busses from Amalfi and Salerno also stop). Coming out of the station, go right to MacDonalds; you will find the stop just beyond this, by the Post Office.

Stage 2: from Naples to your resort
For **Sorrento** take the Circumvesuviana train. If continuing to **Positano**, **Praiano** or **Conca**, take the Amalfi SITA bus outside Sorrento station (tickets from the ground floor bar).

There is an express SITA service from Naples to **Salerno** (€3.10; runs approximately every half hour, Sundays less frequently) which goes by *autostrada*. For travel onward to **Amalfi**, **Ravello**, **Maiori** and **Minori** take the Amalfi bus from the Salerno terminus (tickets here). Alternatively,

---

*At Naples airport you may be in time for the direct bus service to Sorrento (Timetable 15) or Salerno (Timetable 14).

before buying your ticket at Naples, check if one of the infrequent Naples-to-Amalfi direct services is about to leave.

Pronunciation guide

Italian pronunciation follows that of English with a few exceptions. As examples, simple English words are used below:

Vowels

a as in bank
e as set (short) or as the '*a*' in way (long)
i as the 'ea' in leap
o as in hot (short) or as in go (long)
u as the 'oo' in fool.

All vowels are pronounced separately so that, for example, 'aereo' has four syllables.

Consonants

c } are pronounced soft if followed by the vowel
g } 'e' or 'i' (respectively, as the 'ch' in church; as
sc } the 'j' in joke; as the 'sh' in show). If followed by another vowel or a consonant, they are pronounced hard (as the 'k' in king; as 'g' in god; as 'sc' in school).
h is not pronounced.
z is pronounced 'dz' or 'tz'.

Stress

The stress usually comes on the next to the last syllable, e.g. Amalfi. If it comes on the last syllable, the word will have an accent, as in città. Sometimes the stress is made on another syllable and for place names in our area the index shows the stress if not on the next to last syllable.

The inner man

In the main towns of the region you will, of course, find a wide selection of grocers (*alimentari*), confectioners (*pasticceria*), ice cream bars (*gelateria*), bars and restaurants. One of the delights of a holiday, especially if you have bed and breakfast accommodation, is trying out a new restaurant in the evening. Since the local population loves to eat out too, there is a fine selection of restaurants, often in the most unlikely places.

Out of town, in the villages, you can normally reckon on finding only a bar, for drinks, snacks and ice cream. They are often closed during the afternoon siesta

Olive grove at Pantano (junction of Walk segments 47, 48, 49 and 50)

period. It is my impression that the very best cappuccino is served in the smaller villages — strong coffee, creamy foaming top, with dark bitter chocolate sprinkled to taste.

Your other preoccupation with food will be to get the makings of a picnic together, another delight. You can buy bread rolls and fillings from the *alimentari* and fruit from a fruit and vegetable stall. Bread rolls *(panini)* are ordered by number but priced by weight and, if the shop is sold out, they will cut off as much bread as you need from a larger loaf. Cheese and other products are sold by the *etto* (= 100gm; plural *etti*) or the *chilo* (= kilo, same pronunciation). Ham is sold by the *fetta* (= slice; plural *fette*). The *alimentari* will usually slice the roll and fill it for you, if asked. Shop hours are approximately 08.00-13.00 and 17.00-20.00. Don't forget to get your Sunday picnic the evening before; shops are usually not open Sunday mornings.

If you want to add a little extra flavour to your lunch, look for the trays and bottles of pickled and marinated vegetables. Olives are another regional speciality. Some pickled aubergine in your roll will make you lick your lips (and wipe your chin). If your Italian is not up to scratch, just point to what you want.

Flora and fauna

The wild flowers are a treat. Not only do they grow alongside the mountain paths, but the well-paved byways between and in villages also provide a constant feast — flowers

Valerian brightens this path among lemon groves between Atrani and Ravello (Excursion 4 and Walk segment 3).

thrive on the many patches of spare ground and in the crevices of paving and stone walls.

Research for the guide has taken place in all seasons except high summer and in each month the quantity and range of flowers were outstanding. Here is a list of ones we could put a name to: rosemary, white heather, cyclamen, crocus, orchids (incl. bee and monkey), poppy, freesia, cistus, buttercup, spurge, squill, thyme, mint, geranium, various lilies including asphodel, trefoil, broom, garlic, valerian, vetches, honeysuckle.

Cultivated flowers also enliven the scene, growing in window-boxes and gardens. Bougainvillea flowers into December; the scent of jasmine pervades the paths. You will see an array of vegetables and fruit, including many vines. An abiding memory from our May visits is the almost overpowering scent of lemon blossom infusing the air of the terraces. Lemons hang in plump profusion through winter into spring, to be picked well past the time of flowering for the next crop. In winter black nets (as seen at the bottom of the photograph below) are draped over the citrus terraces as a protection against frost and hail.

In contrast to the flora, the region is less rich in fauna. You will probably meet mules and some herded goats and sheep, while in summer and autumn the paths are alive with butterflies and lizards.

If you are out in the mountains in summer, you might well see a snake on the path, sunning itself. Like adders in the UK, they are poisonous but will move away as you approach.

The footpaths — their nature and origin

Given the steep terrain, it is little wonder that many of the footpaths consist of flights of steps. However, what may be surprising is their high standard of construction, for they are much broader than needed for today's light traffic, and mostly they use well-dressed stone. Often, on leaving the alleyways of the town, the path is no less well built as it makes its way through the countryside to the next village, and street lamps often continue.

These street lamps can be useful when route finding. If you are wondering whether a particular path is one of the public ways, then look for street lamps as a sign — though it may seem strange to see a lamp-lit path leading through olive groves! Another sign of the old public ways is the presence of manhole covers. (The word *fognatura* cast into the covers means sewage. The other name often seen, *Cassa per il Mezzogiorno*, is the name of a former state bank, used to channel economic aid to the poor south of Italy; *mezzogiorno* = south.)

Although I have asked many people, no one seems to know for sure anything about the origin of these paths. Nothing is written about them. One view, probably correct, is that since the region has a long and illustrious history of intense economic activity dating back to the early Middle Ages, a well-founded road

Even today, building materials are sometimes brought up the stepped path from Maiori by horses or mules (Walk segments 41 and 46).

network has long been needed. As the terrain is so steep and much of the traffic would have consisted of pack animals, well-made paths were essential. Earthen roads would have become impassable very quickly. Hence the network of tracks paved with stone.

When the motor car burst on the scene, conventional roads were needed. Fortunately, the path network — often consisting as it does of steps — proved unsuitable for modification and so was left alone. Thus the motor roads have been pushed through new ground. This is important to us because, when a path comes up to a road, we can confidently expect the path to cross it and continue on the other side. It is rare to be forced by meeting a road to have to walk along it.

Finally in this section, a word of warning. Marvellous though these paths are for the keen walker, they are held in little regard by the local population. The people responsible for promoting tourism are only now beginning to put value on a wonderful and possibly unique resource. In this age of the internal combustion engine, the paths are little used any more by the local people. A consequence is that, should you ask the way, as like as not you will be directed along the nearest motor road and away from the footpaths. So *be sceptical about route finding advice from the locals,* however charmingly given.

H ints to walkers

The terrain is often extremely steep, so progress is necessarily slow. But the paths are there to be savoured. You find yourself making frequent stops to admire the next view, for photography, or to look into the natural history and villages. Unusual buildings beg to be explored.

For those new to walking. Although the walks described in this guide are for the most part relatively short and follow well-made paths, their steepness may at first seem daunting. Two pieces of advice might prove helpful. First, as all walkers know, the secret of ascending or descending steep paths is to go slowly but to keep going without unnecessary stops. Aim to walk at a pace that allows conversation and smooth breathing. It is all too easy, particularly when going up well built steps, to run out of steam quickly.

Second, when selecting your first walks from your

area walk planner, consider taking shorter routes and those with less climbing and an 'easy' grade. Dip into the 'Excursions with picnic section'. Build up to longer itineraries by stages. Also, look for the bus symbol at higher starting points, and let the bus do the climbing.

What to take

Few of the routes pose any problem from a safety aspect. Civilisation in the form of one's hotel or a bar on a bus route can usually be reached within one hour. Where this is not the case, the walk segment description will give suitable warning.

For **weather protection** it will do to carry a waterproof and warm clothing appropriate to the time of the year. The Lattari mountains seem to attract their own weather, and some rain can be expected in any month from October to May. From December to March you can expect a few cold days, with a daytime temperature at sea level as low as 5°C (41°F), while the mountain tops could get a sprinkling of snow (photograph pages 32-33). Outside these months always take protection from the sun in the form of sun hat and long-sleeved blouse or shirt, and be prepared for the occasional thunderstorm.

For **footwear**, the ubiquitous training or other rubber-soled shoe is ideal. As is clear from the relevant descriptions, on just a few of the walks boots are either required or desirable, in which case the lightweight fabric sort are suitable, except in winter.

If you are walking in warm weather, I cannot stress too much the need to **drink enough water** to avoid dehydration. Err on the copious side. I have drunk as much as four litres on a really hot day when doing a fair amount of climbing. The local water supply is safe so, when you have decided on your route, look in the segment descriptions for the tap symbol (••) to plan your water supply, relying on taps and drinking fountains if possible (take an empty bottle or cup to be able to drink enough when you stop). If you have to carry water, the purchase of a bottle of mineral water on your first day gives a handy container to refill with ordinary tap water on later days. If your bottle has run out and you are passing a house, the request *Per favore, avete acqua da bere?*, showing your bottle, is unlikely to be refused (pair fa**vo**ray, **a**vaytay **ak**wa da **bay**ray?).

The walk planners

As indicated previously, the footpaths of the region form an intricate network and, with the help of the walk planner, you will be able to make your way over them at will. The network has been divided into *segments* running between *key junctions*. For each segment there is an overall description of the landscape and a detailed description of the route. If the segment is described in both directions of walking (as is usually the case), an 'a' or 'b' follows the segment number. Below is a section from the Conca dei Marini planner.

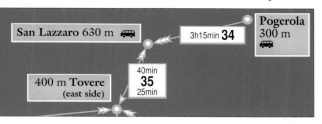

The heights of key junctions are given in metres; a 🚌 symbol indicates whether they are served by bus (you may wish to take the bus to a high junction and walk down). The arrows show whether a description is given for both or only one direction, and the number of arrowheads indicates the grade: easy, moderate, or strenuous. (For example, Walk segment 34 from Pogerola to San Lazzaro is described only in one direction, which is strenuous; Walk segment 35 between Tovere and San Lazzaro is described in both directions, the descent being easy and the ascent moderate.) Walking times for each direction are shown in the box with the segment number (from San Lazzaro down to Tovere allow 25 minutes, from Tovere up to San Lazzaro allow 40 minutes).

Using the planner, you can put together any feasible segments to make up varied routes of the desired length, difficulty and interest. For example, you may have decided to walk from Amalfi to Ravello, intending to return by bus. You could take Walk segment 2 from Amalfi to Atrani, followed by Walk segment 3 from Atrani to Ravello, with total (non-stop) walking time shown by the Amalfi/Ravello area Walk planner as being 1h50min. For the return to Amalfi, instead of travelling by bus you could descend along Walk segments 7 and 6 or 8 and 6. The 'Walk planning tips' for each area suggest some useful combinations of segments.

Grade. This is a measure of the steepness of climbing and the degree to which it is sustained. A segment might rate 'easy' even with quite a lot of climbing if the climbing is spread out into short bursts. It is worth noting that few segments graded 'strenuous' are particularly long and can usually be rendered relatively easy by going slowly and having an occasional rest. Steep descents of more than 200m/660ft are noted, as some people find these hard on the knees and would want to be forewarned.

Walking times are based on my *non-stop* walking times; I walk at an 'average' pace (about 3.5km/2mi per hour). No allowance has been made for major stops. You will need to adjust for your own speed and add in time for picnics and other stops you might make.

The walk segments are divided into six areas, whose limits are defined in the regional map inside the back cover. They are: Amalfi/Ravello, Positano/Praiano, Conca dei Marini, Maiori/Minori, Sorrento, and Capri. The arrangement of walk segments in this edition enables you to put together a **long-distance walk** from Punta Campanella in the west to the Santuario dell'Avvocata in the east: follow (in this order) segments 61, 52, 65, 63, 30, 23, 22, 20, 26, 27, 33, 36, 38, 1, 2, 15, 39 and 46.

Note the following **conventions used in the walk segment descriptions**:

- *Abbreviations; symbol.* CAI: Club Alpino Italiano; AST: Azienda di Soggiorno e Turismo (official tourist office); h: hours; min: minutes; m: metres; ft: feet; km: kilometres; mi: miles; ⟶: tap or drinking fountain.
- Sometimes the path will be described as *'contouring'*. This implies progress along a hillside, either level or with gentle rise or fall.
- *Descriptions given in square brackets* [ ] indicate the connecting points of other segments or minor routes.
- To save space, • indicates a new paragraph; ➡ indicates the ongoing route beyond the point where options join.
- Only the *horizontal* distance is quoted. When you are climbing or descending steps, the distance walked will be longer.

You will see CAI waymarking along a few of the routes in this book, and you may wish to buy the CAI walking map referred to below.

Guides and maps

All national and relevant regional **tourist guides** to Italy feature Sorrento and the Amalfi Coast. They are helpful for general orientation and for a description of the major sights. Once you have arrived, you can buy one of the many colourful descriptive books, for the pictures and for a run-down of local history. The local tourist offices in the major centres can supply you with a colour leaflet, a simple town plan and a list of hotels.

As for **maps**, Kompass No 682 'Penisola Sorrentina' (scale 1:50,000) is good for the overall layout and for motoring. For walking, look for 'Monti Lattari' (scale :30,000) produced by the local Club Alpino Italiano. It consists of the 1953 national survey, updated for roads and overprinted in red (not entirely accurately) with the CAI mountain routes. These are waymarked intermittently on the ground. The contours and rock markings remain accurate, but many footpaths have changed. Mule tracks are more reliable.

Other useful maps available locally

The **Ravell**o tourist office issues free of charge an excellent map of the paths of the **Ravello/Scala/Amalfi** area. Maps by 'Cart&Guide' cover the paths from Maiori to Positano at 10,000 in two sheets. There is also a 'Carta dei Sentiere' available in Positano.

A precise walking map covering the whole **Sorrento nd of the peninsula**, entitled 'Sea of Ulysses, Land of the Sirens — Country Walks', is available free of charge from the Sorrento, Massa Lubrense and Sant'Agata tourist offices. The colour-coding of the walks on the map matches the ceramic tiles at path junctions and the painted waymarks. These routes coincide only partly with the ones chosen for this guidebook.

On Capri look for the 'Capri Trails Map'

✿ Excursions with picnic

There are dozens of ways of spending some delightful hours exploring small villages and out of the way places with little effort or walking, ideal for those hot or lazy days. Here are some suggestions, all of which also have good picnic spots along the way. (For ideas for picnic food, see 'The inner man' on page 11.) Your choice of excursion might let you start straight from your hotel; if not, *travel by public transport is assumed*. Excursions for motorists are described in the Touring section; some of the car tours visit the same places as described below.

Do not think only of outings from your 'home' resort, as bus or boat could easily take you to others.

Excursions from AMALFI

Excursion 1. Spend a couple of hours exploring the tortuous alleys and small piazzas of **Amalfi**. To start with, take Walk segment 1a (photograph pages 24-25), returning along the waterfront (**30min**). Along the way there will be numerous chances to stop for a drink or a meal. A good place to picnic would be at the end of the central pier, sitting on a bench looking back to the town with its mountainous backdrop (photograph pages 34-35).

Excursion 2. Stroll to **Atrani** (Walk segment 2a; **20min**; photograph opposite). Explore its alleys and admire its buildings, often more elegant than those in Amalfi. Picnic by the beach, in the main piazza or, best of all, on the steps of Santa Maria Maddalena (see photographs pages 8 and 40 and the start of Walk segment 3a). Follow Walk segment 2b back to Amalfi (**20min**).

Excursion 3. Take the bus from Amalfi up to the hillside village of **Pogerola**, visit a bar or restaurant (some have super views over the Valley of the Mills), picnic in the small hilltop park near the village centre, look around the old northern part of Pogerola, and then perhaps take Walk segment 4b (**45min**) back down to Amalfi.

Excursion 4. This is a superb all-day excursion which can be taken in easy stages. Although you do have to walk, it goes mostly downhill, can be taken slowly and will absorb your attention with the constantly-changing views. If you are based some way along the coast and can afford only one day in this area, then this excursion is just about the best way of 'doing' **Amalfi and Ravello**.

Take the bus from Amalfi to Ravello. Visit the cathedral and the cathedral museum. Then walk to Villa Cimbrone (**15min**; photographs pages 1, 8). Visit the stunning viewpoint, and look round its wonderfully-sited gardens, with many hidden corners and statuary. It's a lovely place to picnic. A bar operates in summer; there are also restaurants nearby.

Now follow Walk segment 3b from the 'Cimbrone Arch' (see ② at the top of page 43): walk down past the house and descend to Atrani (photograph pages 12-13; **1h**). There is a good picnic spot on the way, on a level stretch after leaving the foot of the Cimbrone cliff. If you have time, explore Atrani's piazza (photograph page 8 and below) and beach, perhaps taking a drink in a bar here, before following Walk segment 2b back to Amalfi (**20min**).

Excursion 5. Take the Agerola bus to **San Lazzaro**; the journey itself provides sensational views of the coast as the bus climbs in many hairpins. From the bus terminus walk down the main street for 100m/yds, turn left and, after another 200m/yds, turn right on a track

On leaving Amalfi, you round a corner and see Atrani nestling under the cliffs (Excursion 2, Walk segment 2).

(sign: 'Castello Lauritano'). Follow this for 600m (0.35mi) to its end — a superb viewpoint high above the Amalfi Coast. On returning to San Lazzaro, it's worth exploring the village. (**30min**).

Excursions from RAVELLO

Excursion 6. In **Ravello** there are two centrally-located picnic spots. From the main square take the broad stepped alley to the left of the cathedral. In 100m/yds, at its top, turn left (Via Toro). The first picnic place is in a small park on the left. The second lies 100m further along, on the right — the *Belvedere Principessa Margherita*, with a stunning view down to the coast (**10min**).

Excursion 7. For a splendid quiet stroll in **Ravello**, with 5-star views and much of interest, see the 'Walk planning tip' at the start of Walk segment 3. This will lead you to a path under the cliff on which the Villa Cimbrone is situated and then back to the alleys of Ravello. The walk takes **40min**, but you will want to linger. You could visit the Villa Cimbrone (see Excursion 4) or picnic en route. Photograph pages 42-43.

Excursion 8. The path from Ravello down to **Minori** (see Walk segment 5a) makes an easy, pleasant stroll and takes about **1h**. You pass through Torello, one of the few villages in the region without a road, and the mountains provide a wonderful backdrop. Once in Minori, you could visit the Roman villa and picnic in the shade of the Piazza Cantilena, finishing with an ice-cream at de Riso's *gelateria*. If you need to return to Ravello, take buses via Amalfi (or by alighting at the junction of the Ravello road east of Atrani).

Excursion from MINORI or MAIORI

Excursion 9. Follow Walk segment 39 from Minori to Maiori, or vice versa (**1h** either way). Halfway along, you could picnic overlooking the sea in the fine little piazza by the church of **San Michele** (photograph page 90). In Minori the best place to picnic is in the shady Piazza Cantilena near the eastern end of the sea-front.

Excursion at CONCA DEI MARINI

Excursion 10. Take the bus to **Conca dei Marini** (alight at the Hotel Belvedere bus stop). From here you follow the start of Walk segment 36b, to two superb viewpoints, looking either way along the coast; you might like to picnic at one of them. (The view east along the coast is shown on page 81.) You can visit the church of San Pancrazio, which lies between the viewpoints. Return to the hotel. A path beside the hotel descends to the beach and bar/restaurants at Spiaggia di Conca. Total walking time is about **50min**.

Excursions from POSITANO

Excursion 11. From Positano take the bus up to **Monte Pertuso** (photograph page 32). Look around the village, picnic in the church piazza or visit a bar or restaurant, and then perhaps take Walk segment 19b to stroll back to Positano (**1h**).

Excursion 12. From Positano take the Monte Pertuso bus up beyond the village to its terminus at **Nocelle**. Walk through the village (bar/restaurant) and down to its finely-situated church piazza, a shady picnic spot. From here return to Monte Pertuso (Walk segment 20b;

Excursion 17: Picnic here at the summit of Monte Solaro, from where there is a superb panorama of Capri and the Bay of Naples. The wild flower meadows just below the summit are exquisite. These three offshore rocks are called the Faraglione islets.

30min) or descend to Positano (Walk segment 21a; **1h30min**) — steps take you down a wild mountainside with views along the coast and down over the Positano. At one time these steps were Nocelle's only link with civilisation.

Excursions from SORRENTO

Excursion 13. From Sorrento, take the bus up to **Termini** (photograph page 9). Follow Walk segment 53a for **5min**, to the super picnic spot shown on pages 26-27 — a grassy mound with distant all-round views. Return to Termini and then descend to **Nerano** (Walk segment 58a; **25min**) and to the fine beach at **Marina del Cantone** (Walk segment 60a; **25min**). The bars and restaurants here are open all year round. Perhaps wander round the headland to Recommone and back (Walk segment 60; **30min**; photograph page 115). Return by bus from Marina del Cantone.

Excursion 14. From Sorrento, take the Massa Lubrense bus or the yellow town bus to **Capo**. Follow Walk segment 48 down to the Roman **Villa di Pollio** and picnic with a fine view of the Bay of Naples. **1h** round trip from Capo.

Excursion 15. From Sorrento, take the Circumvesuviana train to Castellamare di Stabia station, to connect with the cable car to the 1131m/3700ft-high summit of **Monte Faito**. The walk from here to the summit of the highest of the Lattari mountains is described in the book Update available free from www.sunflowerbooks.co.uk.

Excursions on CAPRI

Excursion 16. Both the **Villa Jovis** (Walk segment 66; **1h15min** round trip) and the **Arco Naturale** (Walk segment 67; **50min** round trip) offer good picnic spots. On the way you will enjoy good views of the island from Capri's jasmine scented alleys. Bar/restaurants are en route in both segments. Photograph page 124.

Excursion 17. Take the bus to **Anacapri**. Look around this delightful small town and then take the chair-lift up to the summit of **Monte Solaro**, the setting shown above.

⬤ Touring

If you are undecided about taking your own car or hiring one, *do* give some thought to motoring in the region. Parking in the towns is very difficult and the driving is hectic: most roads are full of bends … fitting perhaps in the country that invented spaghetti. Remember that public buses offer a cheap and efficient alternative means of transport — while at the same time letting you enjoy the scenery as you go.

If, however, you *have* decided to motor in the region, the seven short tours described on the following pages will take you to some out-of-the-way places, fine picnic spots and splendid viewpoints. You will probably also use the car to visit some famous sites outside the area covered by this book — Pompei or Paestum for example — but it is assumed that you will use a road map or atlas to get there; no touring notes are included in this book.

The 'backbone' route of our region is the main road east out of Sorrento: this connects with the SS (Strada Statale) 163, which goes south to the coast and then east all the way to Salerno — the world-famous Amalfi Drive. This coast road, not described in detail here because it is so well signposted, is a dramatic 45km-long corniche, passing through Positano, Vèttica Mag-

Viewed from one of Amalfi's piers, we see how buildings, topped by the chapel of San Biagio, cling to the cliffs, high above the coast road. Walk segment 1 follows the balcony path beside them.

giore, Praiano, Conca dei Marini, Amalfi, Atrani, Minori and Maiori, before heading east to Vietri sul Mare and Salerno.

The first two tours comprise circuits easily accessible from Sorrento. The other tours consist of mostly short excursions starting from various points along the coast road. See the fold-out area map inside the back cover.

The best map for touring the area is the Kompass map No 682, Penisola Sorrentina. All the yellow and the wide white roads shown on this map can be driven, plus some of the narrow white roads.

The following motoring hints apply particularly to the coast road:

- In hold-ups, be sure to come to a halt well to the right, leaving maximum space for a coach to get past and leaving some space behind the car in front in case he needs to back up.
- Be aware of the practice of SITA bus drivers to slow down when the road ahead is clear, to let cars overtake.
- Where there is no official parking area, you may have to park in a sensible spot on a road some way out of town and walk in.

Tour 1: CIRCUIT FROM SORRENTO

This tour is only 37km/23mi long, but there is so much to enjoy you may wish to split it into two days. The tour describes a circuit from Sorrento. Various side-trips are included, to take you to the most interesting locations in the area — where you can perhaps walk or picnic.

Suggestions for stretching your legs: Walk segments 53a, 57 (Walk segment 60 is accessible on a detour to Marina del Cantone)

Leave Sorrento by heading west, and follow signs to **Massa Lubrense** (6km ✝ ▲ ✕ 🎥). It's worth looking around this elegant old town. Back in your car, continue up the wide main street and go left behind the triangle at the top. Follow the road for 1.4km more to a sharp left bend. Here fork right (signposted to Termini) through the village of **Santa Maria** (7km ✝).

Just 0.4km beyond Santa Maria turn right to enter the little village of **Annunziata** (8km ✝ ▮ 🎥). Park and explore on foot (see notes in Walk segment 57 and photograph on page 111). Then return to the road, turn right, and continue downhill. After crossing a bridge, turn left onto a more major road. Drive up through **Termini** to the top end of the village, by the church (12km ✝ ✕ ▲ 🎥). The notes for Walk segment 53a would take you to the picnic spot shown below.

Leave Termini with the church on your left, immediately turn right at the T-junction, and drive ahead up the hillside, zigzagging to the summit ridge. Park and walk left to the hilltop church of **San Costanzo** (✝ 🎥; photograph page 116), to see the whole peninsula laid out before you. Continue by car or on foot west along

the road to its end, for a superb view of Capri out in the glittering sea.

Drive back to Termini and continue out of the village, leaving the church on your left. *Possible detour:* In just 0.4km you could turn right down to Nerano and Marina del Cantone (♣✕) with its fine beach. See the notes in Walk segment 60 and the photograph on page 115. The main tour continues to **Sant'Agata** (20km ♣✕▲▲). From the central T-junction, with the Hotel delle Palme on your left, drive towards the large old church and past it for 0.5km to the gates of **Deserto Convent** (♣📷). Park here and walk up the drive. See the notes at the start of Walk segment 55, to reach the beautiful belvedere here. The old church passed on the way up is worth a visit for its wonderful inlaid marble altars.

Now with the Hotel delle Palme behind you, drive away and after 0.5km turn right at a T-junction with a main road. After 1.6km, at a right hand bend, turn right (signposted 'Eliporto Pineta'). Take the first left (after 0.5km) by a restaurant (✕) and continue for 1km more, to the end of a pine wood on your left. Here at **Capo di Mondo** (📷) the panorama is magnificent, a fine place to enjoy a picnic. Return the way you came and turn right at the main road.

Descend to the next village, **Colli di Fontanelle** (28km, car park on the left). From the car park, walk for about 500m/yds to the right along a narrow road (Via Rocca) that starts level and then climbs gently to reveal ever more dramatic views of Vesuvius and the Bay of Naples. Return the same way to your car. Drive out of the car park, turn right on the main road, retrace your incoming route for 100m, and then turn left downhill on a narrow road (Via Belvedere). After about 1km you reach a small car park with a fine view (📷) along the coast to Positano and the highest mountains of the peninsula beyond it.

Return to Colli di Fontanelle car park and turn left (east) on the main road to drive in 2km to a crossroads (31km). Turn left and follow signs to Sorrento (37km).

The grassy mound at the end of this track near Termini offers far-reaching views; it's a lovely picnic spot (Tour 1, Excursion 13, Walk segments 52 and 53). Capri lies off the shore.

Tour 2: SANTA MARIA DEL CASTELLO AND MONTE FAITO

This circuit (60km/37mi) takes quiet but good roads full of hairpin bends to climb into the mountainous spine of the peninsula. En route is the superb picnic spot shown below, with a fantastic view down to the coastline by Positano. Do not choose this tour if the cloud is low.

Suggestion for stretching your legs: Walk segment 23

From Sorrento take the main road east, signposted to Napoli. Just beyond **Meta** (6km) you leave the towns and start to climb, with the sea on your left. Having rounded the headland and started to descend, after 1km (at the apex of a hairpin bend to the left) turn right into a side road signposted to Monte Faito. Climbing now, pass through **Fornacella** (10km), **Arola** (13km 📷; stop here for fine views down to the Sorrento plain), and **Preazzano** (14km).

Some 4km further on, take the first right turn signposted to **Santa Maria del Castello**. The road climbs in bends up to this church on a promontory (19km ✝️✗📷), from where there is a wonderful all-round view. To picnic in the setting shown below, park at the end of a low wall beyond the church. From here a path leads through a meadow; after 100m/yds it turns right, then left, to the viewpoint. You might also like to walk from the church to the Caserma (barracks) Forestale and back (Walk segment 23).

Return by car down to the main valley road (21km) and turn right to **Moiano** (22km). Here turn right to climb the road up to summit of **Monte Faito** (29km; 1131m/3700ft 📷) and on to the higher summit of **San Michele** (32km; 1278m/4200ft ✝️📷). The road ends here; return the same way to Moiano (42km) and here turn right to descend to **Vico Equense** (50km). Now follow signposting back to Sorrento (60km).

From the promontory church of Santa Maria del Castello you can quickly walk to this superb picnic spot, high above Positano (Tour 2).

Tour 3: MONTE PERTUSO AND NOCELLE

A 6km round trip from the coast at Positano; see town plan page 59
Suggestion for stretching your legs: Walk segment 20

L eave the coast road near the western end of Positano on a narrow road signposted to **Monte Pertuso** (♠✕🖼). This lovely little village (2km), with a well-sited church, bar and restaurants is shown on page 32. You can drive further up the road to where it ends and explore the equally pleasant village of **Nocelle** (♠✕ 🖼), always with the most stunning of views.

Return the same way.

CHIMING CLOCKS
An attractive feature of the towns and villages, particularly on the Amalfi Coast, is the timekeeping provided by one of the local churches in each place. The time is rung out day and night at quarter- hour intervals and can be read by listening to the chimes of the two bells, which follow a code. No doubt you will want to work out the code for yourself, but, if you are still puzzled: one bell chimes the clock hour; another, with a different tone, the quarter-hour (one chime = quarter; two = half, etc; the full hour might get four chimes or be silent). Usually the hour chime comes before the quarter-hour chime, but in a few churches it chimes the other way round.

Tour 4: THE AGEROLA PLAIN

This 46km/29mi tour on minor zigzagging roads crosses the Agerola Plain (600m/1970ft above Amalfi) and affords tremendous views towards the higher mountains and down over the coast.

You can stretch your legs near Il Casino and San Lazzaro; see text.

Leave the coast road 2km west of Amalfi, following signposting for Agerola and Napoli. The road zigzags sensationally uphill for 10km to the first village on the Agerola Plain, **Bomerano** (12km).

Beyond the one-way section, keep right and continue to the next village, **Pianillo** (13.5km ☜). From here quiet roads take you to superb viewpoints and picnic spots. The first visits a viewpoint down to Positano, the second leads to a view over Amalfi and the interesting village of San Lazzaro.

After passing the fine church in Pianillo follow signposting to Napoli; you are directed left at two points. Just 100m after the second bend, where the main road sweeps to the right in a wide arc, turn left on a minor road and, after 150m, turn right. This road now leaves Pianillo and heads northwest, then south, and finally

---

MAJOR SIGHTS OUTSIDE THE REGION

Pompei and Herculaneum. These two world-famous Roman cities were destroyed by volcanic ash from an eruption of Vesuvius, their remains preserved by the same ash and excavated. To reach them from Sorrento, just take the Circumvesuviana train directly to either site (Herculaneum = *Ercolano*). From the Amalfi Coast you could go by bus or boat to Sorrento to pick up the train or join a locally-organised excursion.

Vesuvius. Last erupting in 1944, it has been completely dormant since. A walk around the summit crater on a clear day offers fantastic views. To get there: the local taxi cooperative at Herculaneum station offers a shared minibus service costing €10 return, typically taking a group of people arriving by train. From the summit car park you have a 200m/600ft climb to the rim (€6 access fee). Sensible timings allow a good viewing.

Paestum. This evocative ancient Greek site (shown opposite), with three well-preserved Doric temples and a fine museum, rises in a pastoral setting near the coast south of Salerno. You can get here easily from Salerno. A number of bus operators combine to provide a half-hourly service from the Piazza Concordia, on the sea-front below the main station (journey time approximately 1h). Ask the driver to drop you at Paestum, as there is no signposted bus stop. To be picked up for the return, just hail the bus on the other side of the road junction where you were dropped off.

west, climbing gradually up the lower slopes of the mountains, until it ends 6km from Pianillo, high up above the coast at a place called **Il Casino**. As there is virtually no traffic, you can picnic and walk wherever you like — the views are superb. Then return down the same road to Pianillo.

When you reach the main road again, turn left and continue for another 0.6km, until a road tunnel is visible ahead. Turn right just before the tunnel and follow a high-level minor road above the village of Campora. You enjoy wide views across the plain and to the highest mountains of the peninsula. Just before San Lazzaro, on coming to a T-junction 5km beyond Campora, turn right. Park 200m further on, by the entrance to a track on your left (sign: Castello Lauritano'). Follow this for 600m/0.35mi to a superb viewpoint high above the Amalfi coast.

Return to your car and continue down to **San Lazzaro** (30.5km 🛉). Then follow the signs back to Bomerano and Amalfi (46km).

The classical Greek site of Paestum, south of Salerno, and (inset) a mosaic of Jonah and the whale on a pulpit in the cathedral at Ravello.

Naples. With all the delights of the countryside at hand and other famous sights to see — perhaps thinking, too, of Naples' fearsome reputation — you might be disinclined to spend time there. But if you can fit it in, you will be taken by its vibrant if anarchic street life, crumbling churches and monuments, and, of course, the archaeological museum, an establishment of world importance. With common sense, you and your (minimal) possessions will survive unscathed. Take a lead from one of the conventional guide books.

Tour 5: POGEROLA

A 9km round trip from Amalfi.
Stretch your legs by exploring the village and its hilltop park.

Head west from Amalfi and, after 2km, take the Agerola road (as in Tour 4). After 1km, at the third hairpin bend, turn right for **Pogerola** (4.5km ✕🕮). There are bars and restaurants in this splendid little village (some of them overlooking the Valley of the Mills). The hilltop park, where you could picnic, affords panoramic views.

Tour 6: PONTONE

A 7km round trip from Amalfi; may be combined with a visit to Ravello.
Suggestion for stretching your legs: Walk segment 16

Take the coast road east from Amalfi, through Atrani (photograph page 21). After 1km, turn left for Ravello. Follow this road for 2km; then, just after a hairpin bend to the right, turn left on a side-road signposted to **Pontone** (✝✕🕮). Park after just under 1km, *before* the village. Walk up to the little piazza shown on page 47, with its bar and view down to Amalfi; you could picnic here. *Do* consider doing Walk segment 16 — it's spectacular, as you can see in the photograph on page 56.

Below left: Looking towards Monte Pertuso, high above Positano (Tour 3, Excursion 11, Walk segments 19, 20, 22). Below right: Walking along the ridge that leads to the Santa Maria di Tramonti cemetery, a wonderful

Tour 7: TRAMONTI

This 31km tour takes you from Ravello to Maiori on roads that ring the Tramonti Plain, with a visit to a hilltop cemetery and a wonderful view across to Vesuvius.

Stretch your legs by walking the ridge shown in the photograph below.

The Tramonti Plain lies north of Maiori, ringed by rugged mountains (see description in Walk segment 43). From the tunnel under Ravello, go left on the road signposted to Valico Chiunzi, gradually climbing the hillside. Some 7km uphill, watch for the road descending right, signposted 'Pietre/Polvica'.

Follow this road downhill for 2km, to where a wide road goes left. Turn onto this and follow it for 1km, to the village of **Capitignano**. Continue through the village, gradually ascending to a cemetery, **Santa Maria di Tramonti** (12km; photograph below). Enjoy the views down to the villages of Tramonti and up to the encircling mountains. Then retrace your route back up to the Valico Chiunzi road.

Now turn right; after 2.5km you reach a crossroads at the crest of the main mountain ridge (19km). Enjoy the view across to Vesuvius, perhaps from the terrace of the nearby restaurant. From here follow the Maiori road for 12km, back to the coast at **Maiori** (31km).

viewpoint with the Tramonti Plain at your feet and a ring of high rugged mountains (Tour 7; Walk segment 44). Poles like those shown are used all over the region to support vines and lemon trees.

❋ Amalfi/Ravello

In common with most of the Costiera Amalfitana (Amalfi Coast), this area is one of high mountains rising steeply out of the sea, riven by deep gorges. Limestone cliffs abound. The natural vegetation is woodland, giving way to grass on the higher slopes but, where the gradient relents in the lower parts, the hillside is terraced for olives, vines, vegetables and, of course, the famous Amalfi lemons. This region has not suffered the depopulation of lands further north so, for the most part, the terraces are kept in pristine condition. They reach into seemingly impossible places, making you wonder how farmers get to them or carry the produce out.

The area comprises three major valleys, those leading into Amalfi (Valle dei Mulini), into Atrani (Valle del Dragone) and into Minori (Valle del Sambuco). Additionally, a short but perilously steep gorge falls from Pogerola to the sea (Vallone Cieco). Wild rocky promontories separate the valleys; at the top of the most easterly of them lies the town of Ravello. The Lattari mountains form the backdrop to the area and frequently rise to over 1000m/3300ft; the highest peak in the Amalfi/Ravello region is Monte Cerreto, at 1316m/4300ft.

Getting about

Buses. The main SITA bus station is located on the sea-front in Amalfi, with a summary of the timetables posted outside and a copy of the main timetables available inside. Tickets can be bought here. Typical fares are shown on page 133. The principal routes from Amalfi go to Salerno; Positano and Sorrento; Ravello and Scala; Pogerola; Agerola (for Bomerano and San Lazzaro). See timetables on page 129.

Amalfi from the central pier, a good spot for a picnic (Excursion 1). The blue SITA buses can be seen at the station; boats leave from the this pier.

34

Boats. Conventional boats and jet boats take you (Easter to end-October) to Positano, Capri, Sorrento and (all year) to Salerno. Compared with bus travel, fares are higher, but journey times shorter. Pick up timetables from the harbour kiosks.

Tourist sights

Amalfi. The classical Roman and Greek civilisations passed Amalfi by but, come the early Middle Ages, its power had grown mightily. In its heyday as a maritime trading republic it rivalled Venice, Pisa and Genoa. A code of maritime law, the 'Tavola Amalfitana', originated in Amalfi and through the inventor, Flavio Gioia, it gave the western world the magnetic compass.

Today, Amalfi (pop. 6500) plays an unassuming role as regional centre. It takes the tourist onslaught easily in its stride and bustles about its own business in a cheerful open fashion. The town itself has grown over the centuries in a higgledy-piggledy way, with houses piled upon each other, making use of every last square centimetre of space, served by a rabbit-warren of stone-paved alleys.

The major sights are: the cathedral of Sant'Andrea, with its brilliant façade (photograph page 44), Baroque interior, and crypt with a relic of St Andrew; Cloisters of Paradise; armoury; town museum; many old chapels; working paper mill; cemetery (the colonnaded building that dominates the eastern side of town); several small beaches.

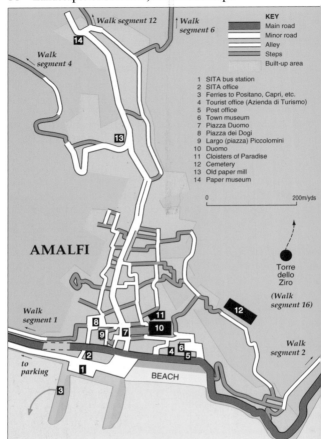

KEY
Main road
Minor road
Alley
Steps
Built-up area

1 SITA bus station
2 SITA office
3 Ferries to Positano, Capri, etc.
4 Tourist office (Azienda di Turismo)
5 Post office
6 Town museum
7 Piazza Duomo
8 Piazza dei Dogi
9 Largo (piazza) Piccolomini
10 Duomo
11 Cloisters of Paradise
12 Cemetery
13 Old paper mill
14 Paper museum

Festivals: An Easter procession wends its way from the cathedral through a torch-lit town at 8pm on Good Friday. Every fourth year (the next will be in June 2009) Amalfi hosts the 'Regatta of the Four Ancient Maritime Republics', a superb spectacle that commemorates Amalfi's former glory. It rotates annually between Amalfi, Pisa, Genoa and Venice.

Ravello. In history, Ravello mirrors Amalfi, as its economic power and influence peaked at about the same time, the Rufolo family being the driving force. The town (pop. 2500) is now quite different from Amalfi in that it is much smaller, being little more than a village, and is spread out over its hilltop setting with

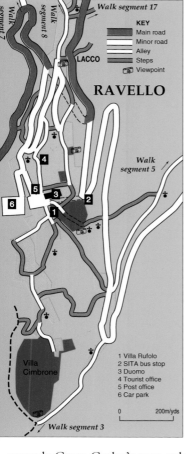

KEY
Main road
Minor road
Alley
Steps
Viewpoint

LACCO

RAVELLO

Walk segment 17

Walk segment 7

Walk segment 8

Walk segment 5

Walk segment 3

Villa Cimbrone

1 Villa Rufolo
2 SITA bus stop
3 Duomo
4 Tourist office
5 Post office
6 Car park

0   200m/yds

a multitude of gardens and floral walkways.

The major sights are: the cathedral, with an austere interior, sloping floor and fancifully-large pulpits (photograph page 31); the cathedral museum (downstairs) has a number of relics and some splendid mosaics; old chapels; the villas Rufolo (13th century) and Cimbrone (19th century, in Moorish style) — both have enchanting gardens, laid out in the late 19th century by a Scotsman and an Englishman, respectively. The Villa Cimbrone is a 'must' because of its large gardens, resplendent with statues in a spectacular setting. A plaque let into a wall (photograph page 1) records Greta Garbo's stay, when she was rescued by Leopold Stokowski from the clamour of Hollywood to spend times of 'joyful secrecy' at Cimbrone.

Atrani. This small fishing village (photograph page 21) resembles Amalfi's baby sister in situation and character. The analogy may be carried further: blood relations do not always get on well, and there is some rivalry between the two communities. A fruitful hour or two can be spent exploring its delightful piazza, tortuous alleys, elegant old buildings and the dramatically-situated church of Santa Maria Maddalena shown on pages 8, 40 and 55. Small stony beach; good restaurants and bars.

Walk Planning Tips

A lovely combination from Amalfi which, taken slowly, can fill a delightful day, comprises segments 12a, 16 and 6b. Enjoy your picnic by the Torre dello Ziro. See also Excursions 1 to 5.

Out of area walks: Amalfi has the bus and boat connections to make all the walks in the guide reachable for a day's excursion. Two outstanding expeditions, starting from Bomerano in Agerola are Walk segments 28a and 27a and Walk segments 28a, 26a, 20b and 19b. For a stylish way to end the last walk take the boat from Positano back to Amalfi. Or take Walk segment 34 from Pogerola to San Lazzaro in Agerola, which gives access to the segments in the Conca dei Marini area.

WALK SEGMENTS

1 Amalfi — road tunnel (west end)

This is a traffic-free means of reaching the western end of the Amalfi road tunnel, from where three further segments radiate. It is also an enjoyable stroll in its own right. The middle part of the route gives wide views back to the town and down to the sea-front. The route follows a track parallel to the main coast road, initially high above it, later outside the tunnel.
Photograph pages 24-25

1a Amalfi (Piazza Duomo) to the road tunnel (west end)
Time: 15min; *Grade:* easy, with a *height gain* of 50m/160ft

With your back to the cathedral, go half-right across the piazza and under the archway by a jewellers, to enter another piazza (dei Dogi). From the far left-hand corner of this piazza, ascend steps (Salita San Nicola dei Greci). Shortly, turn left up more steps. Continue ascending between and under houses, until the path levels out and fine views open up. Note the buildings set into the cliff-side and a minuscule chapel (Santissima Annunziata). Continue to the road at the tunnel entrance. Cross over and take the path outside the tunnel to its far (western) end. [From here a set of steep steps leads down to the sea-front and breakwater, with good views of Amalfi. Return along the sea-front.]

1b Road tunnel (west end) to Amalfi (Piazza Duomo)
Time: 15min; *Grade:* easy, with a *height gain* of 20m/65ft

Take the path that runs outside the tunnel. On reaching the road again, cross it and take the path up to the right. Follow this in an obvious line to the centre of Amalfi.

2 Amalfi — Atrani

A route to Atrani that avoids the busy road and offers a marvellous surprise view of Atrani (when going from Amalfi; photograph page 21). Each end

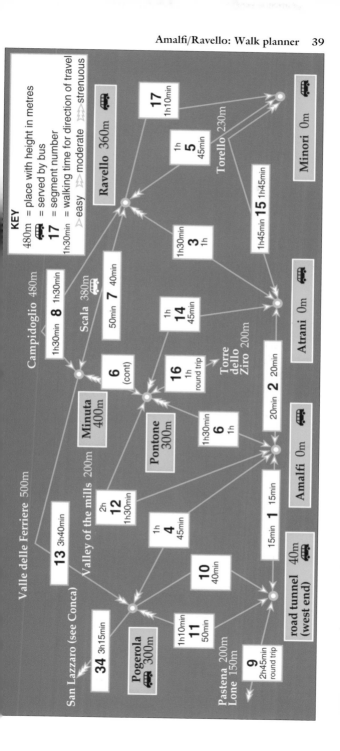

KEY
480m = place with height in metres
🚌 = served by bus
17 = segment number
1h30min = walking time for direction of travel
▷ easy ▷▷ moderate ▷▷▷ strenuous

Church of Santa Maria Maddalena in Atrani

*of the route sees the path taking a tortuous track between and under old houses. **Photograph page 21***

2a Amalfi (Piazza Duomo) to Atrani (Piazza Umberto)

Time: 20min; *Grade:* easy, with a *height gain* of 50m/160ft

Take the lesser steps up alongside and to the left of the main cathedral steps. At their top, turn right under the cathedral and then left, along a dark narrow passage, to a small square which opens into a larger square and the coast road. (The town museum is located in the far corner of this square, adjoining the 1st floor administrative offices: medieval costumes, objects and papers to do with Flavio Gioia, inventor of the magnetic compass in Europe; splendid mosaic; the 'Tavola Amalfitana', an ancient code of maritime law.) • On joining the coast road, just past a pedestrian crossing, ascend steps on the left (Salita Roberto il Guiscardo). These quickly turn right to run parallel with the road. They ascend between and under houses and, at the top, bend left to reveal a fine view of Atrani. [Steps up to the left here lead to Amalfi cemetery, the colonnaded building that dominates the eastern slopes of the town.]

• On reaching the houses of Atrani, take the first narrow passage down to the right (Via Don G Colavolpe). After a few zigzags, just before the steps to the road, turn left up a few steps and then start the final descent to Atrani. At each junction go downhill, until you reach the piazza with its drinking fountain.

2b Atrani (Piazza Umberto) to Amalfi (Piazza Duomo)
Time: 20min; *Grade:* easy, with a *height gain* of 50m/160ft

In the Piazza Umberto with its drinking fountain, with your back to the sea, take the narrow dark passageway in the far left corner (by a post box; Via Campo). Shortly, at a T-junction, turn left. The alley curves right and then left, rising between houses. Turn right up Via Torricelli and, shortly, go left at a T-junction. • The path now leads straight ahead into Amalfi and down to the coast road at the end of the main sea-front. Turn right into a small square, then an inner square. Take the passage at the far left corner, which leads to the Piazza Duomo.

3 Atrani — Ravello

*You climb from Atrani on the coast to Ravello high on its ridge by a most interesting route. After leaving the alleys of Atrani and its finely-situated church, the path traverses a cliff high above the coast road. Later it turns inland and runs among lemon and olive groves along a ridge, under the towering outlook of the Villa Cimbrone. Wild flowers (bee orchids and freesias in late March) abound. The views are always outstanding and rapidly-changing. The path takes a long steep flight of steps in its middle section. There is a choice of two routes for the final ascent to Ravello, going left or right to skirt the base of the cliff on which the Villa Cimbrone outlook stands. The descent is equally fine. **Photographs pages 8, 12-13, 42-43 and 55***

Walk planning tip: An excellent easy 40min stroll from Ravello's main square can be made out of the first option in Walk segment 3b, followed by the last part of Walk segment 3a (see the segment descriptions). This route descends east from Ravello below the cliff on which Villa Cimbrone stands, re-entering the town from the west.

3a Atrani (Piazza Umberto) to Ravello (Piazza Vescovado)
Time: 1h30min; *Grade:* strenuous, with a *height gain* of 360m/1180ft

In the Piazza Umberto with its drinking fountain, with your back to the sea, take the far right-hand passage (Via F M Pansa). Shortly after leaving the passage take the flight of steps leading up left and follow these ever upwards to the church Santa Maria Maddalena. • In Largo Santa Maria Maddalena, with your back to the church, take the left-hand exit, up steps. Very shortly turn right (Via Pastina). Climb steps that traverse the cliff-face. Some houses are reached 300m/ yds from the church (•• on right). Take first left, up more steps. • About 40m/yds along, you come to a house with round windows. [**Walk segment 15** takes the level path to the right, in front of this house.] Continue up steps to left of the house, cross the main Ravello road, and ascend a long flight of steps between walls. The path levels out on a ridge which makes a good picnic spot.

(Now a cliff towers above you, topped by the belvedere of the Villa Cimbrone; a little to the right a white house, La Rondinaia, the former home of American writer Gore Vidal, clings to the lip of the cliff; on the next ridge over the valley you see the village of Pontone and, further left, the promontory crowned by the Torre dello Ziro.) • From here ascend more steps, until you reach the base of the cliff. The path levels out and becomes concreted. At this point a path goes sharp left. Here you have a choice of two routes. ① Go right, past the church of Santa Cosma and houses shown below, until you reach a minor road. Turn left. After about 200m/yds, look for steps leading up to the left. Starting with a short zig-zag, take these to the centre of Ravello. Turn right at the top to reach the main square. ② Go sharp left. [The 'Walk planning tip' route goes straight on at this junction.] The path climbs initially and passes lemon groves for 600m/0.35mi, with the cliff rising to the right, until you reach an olive grove. Take concrete steps leading up right, to reach Ravello at the entrance to the Villa Cimbrone. Turn left for the main square some 600m/0.35mi away.

3b Ravello (Piazza Vescovado) to Atrani (Piazza Umberto)
Time: 1h; *Grade:* easy, with a *descent* of 360m/1180ft
Leave the main square towards Hotel Rufolo. Go under a short tunnel. Now you have two options. ① Turn left down Via Orso Papice. This bends right after a few metres and descends gently to a minor road, where you turn right. After 200m/yds, at a hairpin bend, take the

path to the right and contour the foot of the cliff, passing the church of Santa Cosma and houses shown below. When the concrete surface of the path ends, descend steps to the left. [The 'Walk planning tip' route goes straight on at this junction.] ② Follow signs to Villa Cimbrone. After 600m/0.35mi you reach an arch with the name 'Villa Cimbrone' in ceramic tiles. Turn right down steps on the right-hand side of a house (Via Santa Barbara), descending to an olive grove. Turn left along an earthen path, follow it for 600m/0.35mi, and come to a concrete path at the foot of the cliff. Turn sharp right down steps here. ➡ Follow the path down the steps, along a short ridge (super views, described in segment 3a above), and then go left down steep steps between walls. Go straight across the main Ravello road and continue downhill. [Shortly, **Walk segment 15** joins from a level path on the left, by a house with round windows.] • In a further 40m/yds turn right at a T-junction. Pass a ↔ and follow the path straight on, down across the cliff-face, to the church of Santa Maria Maddalena perched on a promontory. Take the path from the corner of the square in front of the church, descending between houses to the Piazza Umberto with its drinking fountain.

4 Amalfi — Pogerola

This path provides an attractive route to or from the hillside village of Pogerola. The easily-graded and exceptionally well-built path is unusual in that it goes through light woodland rather than farmed terraces, with ever-wider views as you gain height. The path wends its way towards the mountains, climbing the northern flank of a side-spur of the main Amalfi valley. Note the quality of design of the steps in the middle part of the walk, which are slightly bowed to left and right to lead rain water to the edges.

Tip: The 'Cocktail Bar' in Pogerola serves top-class cappuccino coffee and wonderfully-bitter chocolate. There is also another bar and a restaurant with views to the mountains. It's worth exploring the small hilltop park and the old section to the north, for the panoramic views.

4a Amalfi (Piazza Duomo) to Pogerola (main square)

Time: 1h; Grade: moderate, with a height gain of 300m/ 980ft

Ascend the main street for 500m/yds, until the road goes through an archway under a block of houses. Then take the side road to the left (Via

Approaching Ravello you pass under this towering cliff, carved out to accommodate some houses and the church of Santa Cosma (Walk segment 3, Excursion 7). The Villa Cimbrone is set at the top of the cliff.

Casamare). Follow this round the hairpin bend to its end. The path starts here with steps, climbing the hillside and ultimately leading directly to the main square in Pogerola.

4b Pogerola (main square) to Amalfi (Piazza Duomo)
Time: 45min; *Grade:* easy

With your back to the drinking fountain in the main square, leave by the alley opposite (by a three-globed street lamp), and turn right immediately, passing the entrance to a restaurant. Follow this path downhill. Turn right in Amalfi down to the Piazza Duomo.

5 Ravello — Minori

This path makes its way at an easy gradient down from the main square in Ravello to the sea-front in Minori, going through the small village of Torello and passing four chapels. It is well built and yields fine views over the surrounding district, with jagged mountains in the distance. The path follows the crest of a minor spur, initially on the landward side and, lower down, on the seaward side. Minori has a wide range of shops, restaurants and bars. The Piazza Cantilena by the basilica near the eastern end of the sea-front is a wonderfully quiet shady spot, maybe for a picnic. Try the top-class ice cream with a wide choice of luscious flavours at de Riso's nearby on the front.

5a Ravello (Piazza Vescovado) to Minori (Piazza Umberto)
Time: 45min; *Grade:* easy

From the main square take the wide alley on the left of the entrance to the Villa Rufolo (Via della Annunziata). Go through a tunnel under the Rufolo gardens. Some 200m/yds from the main square cross a minor road and descend (Via San Pietro) for a further 100m/ yds to a chapel with a large antechamber. • Turn left along a level, then gently descending path (Via Loggetta). After 200m/yds turn right at a T-junction with a ➴. Immediately cross a minor road and enter Torello, reaching its large chapel on the right after 200m/yds. [**Walk segment 15**

The cathedral ('duomo') of Sant'Andrea in Amalfi, overlooked by the ruined Torre dello Ziro (Walk segment 16; see also photograph page 56).

joins here (Via Toretta Marmorata).] • The path continues to descend gradually for 1km/0.6mi, past another chapel and ↦. Nearing Minori, the end of a road is met, with a cemetery on right. Turn right to pass in front of the cemetery and continue down steps. Just before the last flight of steps to the main coast road (by a ↦), go left under a house and take steps down to Minori, crossing the main coast road.

5b Minori (Piazza Umberto) to Ravello (Piazza Vescovado)
Time: 1h; *Grade:* moderate, with a *height gain* of 360m/1180ft

From the Piazza Umberto, at the western end of the sea-front, take Via degli Arsenale to a pedestrian crossing. From here ascend Via S Giovvanni Mare to the main coast road by a ↦. Cross the road and ascend steps up to the main gate of the cemetery. On reaching the end of a road, turn immediately left up the side of the cemetery. Above the cemetery, fork left and climb steps past a further ↦ and a chapel. After 1km/0.6mi you reach the large chapel of Torello on your left. [**Walk segment 15** heads left here (Via Toretta Marmorata).] • Continue ascending between the houses, after 200m/yds crossing a minor road. Immediately turn left along a path, opposite a ↦. After 200m/yds, at a chapel, turn half-right from the far corner of the antechamber. This path ascends to and crosses a minor road to lead directly to the main square in Ravello.

6 Amalfi — Minuta (Scala road hairpin bend), via Pontone

*You take steep steps under cliffs and past lemon groves to Pontone and rather less steeply up to Minuta. Views of the Valle dei Mulini open up rapidly and, after Pontone, Ravello comes into view. Both small old villages occupy outstanding sites, with quiet piazzas and ruins of old fortresses and churches. Pontone and Minuta are strategically situated, as other path segments radiate from them. The segment is equally fine in descent. Pontone has a bar and two restaurants. **Photograph page 47***

Walk planning tip: Having reached the hairpin bend (Minuta), if you have an hour and some energy to spare, consider doing just the first part of Walk segment 13 — as far as the fantastic Bosco Grande viewpoint. Return the same way.

6a Amalfi (Piazza Duomo) to Minuta (Scala road hairpin bend)
Time: 1h30min (Amalfi — Pontone 1h; Pontone — Minuta 30min); *Grade:* strenuous, with a *height gain* of 400m/1300ft

Ascend the main street for 400m/yds until you are just past the narrow one-way section controlled by traffic lights. Here turn right up Salita dei Patroni. The path curves left and levels out. Continue parallel with the road until a house stands straight ahead, graced by a mural of the Immaculate Conception. Take the uphill path to the right of this house, leaving the town. The steps go up under cliffs and zigzag to a junction. Now you have a choice of two routes. ① Go straight ahead along a short level stretch and then very steeply uphill past a few houses. After 200m/yds you reach a three-way junction, where each path passes under an arch. [**Walk segment 12** goes left here.] Turn right for Pontone square with its drinking fountain. ② Turn sharp right, to continue up steps. [When the path finishes curving to the left after 150m/yds, a narrow steep flight of steps goes up to the right, by a red door; this is a short-cut to the Torre dello Ziro path, **Walk segment 16**.] The main path continues directly up to Pontone square. ➡ Continuing up to Minuta, with your back to the Blu Bar, *either* turn right up steps beneath the church of San Filippo Neri *or* go straight ahead for about 100m/yds, then take the next right up steps (by a ➡➡ on the right), passing the newly restored ruin of San Eustachio. • The options converge and lead up to Minuta. On approaching Minuta church from below, do not go straight ahead up narrow steps; instead, turn sharp left to continue on the main path. In the square, go past the drinking fountain on the left and take steps up to reach the motor road at the hairpin bend.

6b Minuta (Scala road hairpin bend) to Amalfi (Piazza Duomo)
Time: 1 h; *Grade:* easy, with a *descent* of 400m/1300ft
From the hairpin bend on the Scala road descend steps directly away from the apex of the bend. These lead to Minuta's square. Continue down to the right, past the drinking fountain. Descending, keep to the main path for 200m/yds, until a fork is reached where the route to the left descends under an arch. Either fork will take you to the square in Pontone, with its drinking fountain. From the square you have two options: ① With your back to the Blu Bar, go straight ahead for about 150m/yds to a three-way junction where each path goes under an arch; turn left here; ② Take steps down to the right of the chapel and to the left of the view point, immediately crossing a minor road. ➡ Both options converge and lead down to Amalfi; the way ahead or down at each junction is obvious.

7 Ravello — Minuta (Scala road hairpin bend), via Scala
This route, largely along the quiet Scala road, is more useful than attractive, as it connects Ravello to other interesting segments, but it does

The piazza in Pontone, with the Blu Bar at the left. This is a junction for walk segments 6, 12, 14 and 16.

give excellent views of Ravello. Scala's cathedral ('duomo'), with its crypt containing 13th-century wooden sculptures, is worth a visit. There are two bars in Scala; also public toilets and a drinking fountain beside the duomo.

7a Ravello (Piazza Vescovado) to Minuta (Scala road hairpin bend)
Time: 50min; *Grade:* easy, with a *height gain* of 80m/260ft
Take the road opposite the *duomo* out of Ravello's main square, descending gradually and passing the road tunnel entrance. At the first hairpin bend turn right along the Scala road. Some 200m/yds beyond the bridge, take the path to the right; this short-cut eliminates two further hairpins. The path leads to Scala. • From here follow the road for another 1km/0.6mi, to the Minuta hairpin bend.

7b Minuta (Scala road hairpin bend) to Ravello (Piazza Vescovado)
Time: 40min; *Grade:* easy
From Minuta take the road gently downhill for 1km/0.6mi to Scala. Some 200m/yds past Scala's cathedral descend steps to the right — a short-cut across two hairpin bends. On reaching the main Ravello road turn left, then go right at the tunnel entrance, up to Ravello's main square.

8 Ravello — Minuta, via Santa Caterina

An alternative to Walk segment 7, this route is preferable, as it involves less road walking and offers panoramic views. It also makes a foray into wild country by contouring into and out of the head of the valley leading up from Atrani (Valle del Dragone), passing through a couple of sleepy villages on the way. Not recommended during heavy rain, as a streambed (usually dry) must be crossed. Cistus and cyclamen will be seen here in May.

Walk planning tip: Coming from Ravello, if you intend to do Walk segment 13, or even just to visit the Bosco Grande viewpoint, take this short cut: in Campidoglio take steps up to the right (signed CAI 57), just before the first bend left in the road. This path soon turns left and contours for 400m/yds, to the prominent four-way junction in Walk segment 13.

8a Ravello (Piazza Vescovado) to Minuta (Scala road hairpin bend)
Time: 1h30min; *Grade:* easy, with a *height gain* of 200m/660ft
From Ravello's main square, take the broad steps up to the left of the *duomo*. At their top, turn left into Via San Giovanni del Toro. Follow this for 200m/yds, then fork

right along an alley (by the Hotel Caruso). After 200m/yds turn right, to reach the end of a road, by a fountain. This is Lacco, the northern satellite of Ravello. • Continue straight ahead between elegant old houses for 150m/yds, to to Piazza Andrea Mansi and a chapel. Now take the very narrow, level road going straight ahead (Via San Trifone). Continue to its end (about 700m/0.4mi from Lacco). Here it ascends a few steps, becomes a wide mule track, and shortly is paved. After 400m/yds on the track, look for a second old lime kiln on the right. Just past this, take a minor earthen path to the left, below the paving, and descend to a T-junction with a wider path. Turn left to a stream crossing by a small concrete dam (the streambed is usually dry). A paved path continues on the other side, gently rising to a small farm. Cross a small bridge and climb steps under a chapel (San Paulo), to reach the road by the church of Santa Caterina. • Cross the road and follow a minor road opposite the church. After about 100m/yds turn right up narrow well-made steps between walls. At a T-junction turn left. Descend steps, then follow a path which generally contours the hillside; at one point the path crosses an asphalt road obliquely. [Shortly after this crossing, well-made steps lead down to Scala.] Some 700m/ 0.4mi along, the path ends by house. Take steps up to a road, turn left for 40m/yds, and turn left again down a more major road in Campidoglio. Follow this gently downhill for 800m/0.5mi to Minuta.

8b Minuta (Scala road hairpin bend) to Ravello (Piazza Vescovado)
Time: 1h30min; Grade: easy, with a height gain of 160m/500ft

From Minuta take the road to the left, climbing gently along the hillside for 800m/0.5mi to Campidoglio. The road sweeps right and then left between houses; where it then steepens, take a paved road obliquely down to the right. After 40m/yds descend a short flight of steps on the right, to a chapel. Here follow a path that contours the hillside for about 700m/0.4mi (at one point you will recross the asphalt road obliquely). • The path climbs up some stone steps; shortly afterwards, with a house straight ahead, turn right down narrow steps between walls. At a T-junction, turn left. After 100m/yds you reach a road with a church opposite (Santa Caterina). • Take the path down to the left of the church, passing under a chapel (San Paulo). Then turn right over the first of two bridges, down past a small farm. Cross a streambed (usually dry) by a small concrete dam. The mule track on the other side bends right, then left. After 50m/yds more, just beyond a tree with a yellow diamond, turn right onto a lesser path. This bends right and ascends to a paved mule track. • Turn right. After 400m/ yds it becomes a narrow road. After another 700m/ 0.4mi you reach a proper road at a small piazza (with a fine view to the east) and an hotel. This is Lacco, the northern satellite of Ravello. Fork left by the fountain and after 50m/yds turn left into an alley. Follow this for 200m/yds to the Hotel Caruso, then continue on a narrow road for another 200m/yds, to where you can turn right to Ravello's main square.

9 Pastena/Lone circuit, from the road tunnel (west end)

Beloved of Longfellow, this hillside to the west of Amalfi, overlooking the sea, is an area of lemon groves and wild flowers. On uniformly good paths, the route visits three finely-situated chapels, including those at Pastena and Lone; they are floodlit and visible at night from Amalfi. The upper part of the circuit has a definite 'mountain' feel about it, and an optional short detour can be made to the edge of cliffs and gorges rising to 700m/2300ft. The segment is described only in an anti-clockwise direction, with the climb (and major points of interest) at the start, followed by an easy descent to Amalfi. **Photograph page 7**

Time: 2h15min (optional detour to Tuoro: add 30min); *Grade:* moderate, with a *height gain* of 250m/820ft

From the west end of the Amalfi road tunnel, take the narrow road (Via Maestra dei Villaggi) that rises gently between apartments. It shortly turns into a path. Follow this for 200m/yds, until you reach the first of the three chapels on the walk (La Carmine); it forms an arch over the path, with a mural of the Flight into Egypt. [**Walk segment 11** goes up the steps to the right, just before the chapel.] • Continue from the arch for 200m/yds, until you come to a ↔. Turn right up Salita Pomicara. The path rises steeply up a gully and then crosses lemon groves for 150m/yds, after which it turns left and levels out. [An earthen path goes right here to connect with segment 11 on its way to/from Pogerola.] • Continue left along the level stretch for 50m/yds, to a bridge. Go left across the bridge and continue for 250m/yds, up to a second chapel with a campanile, at Pastena — a marvellous viewpoint. Continue up the flight of steps from the chapel, cross the Pogerola road and carry on up the hillside to a T-junction with a level path (200m/yds from the chapel). Turn left. • Continue along the foot of the mountains; after 300m/yds, the path descends to a staggered four-way junction in the midst of houses. [Here an optional detour is possible: you can follow the path to the right (Via delle Sorgenti) to its end, to nose into the mountains at a place called Tuoro. Return when the path deteriorates.] • The main circuit continues straight ahead from the staggered junction down an unnamed path (*not* the Via Carammone). On reaching the Pogerola road, cross it and continue down to a third chapel, at Lone, where there is another campanile and fabulous view, as well as a shady plane tree with a seat for a picnic. • From the chapel take steps down to a lower viewpoint with diagonal red-tiled paving. Turn left here: the path leads you straight back to the Amalfi road tunnel after 1km/0.6mi.

10 Pogerola to the Amalfi road tunnel (west end), via Vallone Cieco

This steep and unrelenting path on stone steps makes a dramatic descent from Pogerola to Amalfi. Ascending is not recommended (except for masochists), so only the downward route is described. The path starts descending gently enough between houses, but steepens and winds through olive groves and, finally, a narrow gorge (Vallone Cieco), to reach the coast road at the west end of the tunnel.

Time: 40min; *Grade:* easy, with a *descent* of 280m/920ft
Take the road from the square beside the church in Pogerola. Just before it ends, descend steps on the right. Follow these ever downward; as you come into the gorge, they are very steep indeed. The steps lead directly to the west end of the Amalfi road tunnel.

11 Amalfi road tunnel (west end) — Pogerola, via the western rim of Vallone Cieco

This third route to or from Pogerola connects a couple of other paths that could be useful, but are not important enough to merit description as segments in their own right (these are noted in the text below). After the chapel of La Carmine, the path goes straight up the hillside to Pogerola, leaving the deep cleft of the Vallone Cieco to the right (on the ascent).

11a Amalfi road tunnel (west end) to Pogerola
Time: 1h10min; *Grade:* strenuous, with a *height gain* of 280m/920ft
Follow Walk segment 9 as far as the chapel of La Carmine. Take the steps just before the chapel, leading up to the right. • Follow these up some zigzags and then a straight ascent; after 200m/yds, the path bends left up steps. Here continue to the right, along a level concrete path. [The other path continues to the left. After 50m/yds, steep steps leads up right to the Grand Hotel Excelsior. If, instead of going up these steps, you were to follow the narrow overgrown path ahead (with

street lamps!), it would take you through lemon groves to **Walk segment 9**.] • The concrete path contours through woods and then ascends gradually; after 500m/yds, below the far end of some apartments, descend to the right. Cross a little flat bridge, then continue over level ground for 100m/yds. Some 50m/yds before a house, turn left up steps that ascend steeply to a church seen above (crossing a narrow road en route). Go round the back of the church to reach the main square.

11b Pogerola to the Amalfi road tunnel (west end)

Time: 50min; *Grade:* easy, with a *descent* of 280m/920ft

Take the steps immediately to the left of the drinking fountain in Pogerola's square, descending to a church. Pass behind this, turn right, and then descend steps by an apartment block. Having crossed a narrow road en route, you come to a T-junction: turn right here, cross a flat bridge and then climb a few steps. Now turn left on Via Pietralato, which descends gently through woods for 500m/yds. • The path meets another on a bend [see notes in brackets in segment 11a]. Turn left downhill. Continue down for 200m/yds, to a large path emerging from an arch under a chapel. Turn left here and follow the path for 200m/yds to the Amalfi road tunnel.

12 Valle dei Mulini (Valley of the Mills)

*Amalfi's paper-making industry ('carta bambagina') has been long renowned, relying for water and power on the torrent that rushes from the mountains down the valley behind the town. Sadly, only one of its mills still operates. This walk goes up past some derelict mills, into a valley of sylvan glades and tumbling streams. It is scarcely credible that this route never extends beyond a mile and a half from the town centre, so remote does it feel. The paths are good, with excellent stream-side picnic sites. An attractive continuation to Pontone follows, with super views down to Amalfi from a balcony path. Bar and restaurants in Pontone. **Photograph page 47***

12a Amalfi to Pontone

Time: 2h; *Grade:* easy, with a *height gain* of 300m/980ft

From the Piazza Duomo, follow the main street up beyond the one-way section, through the arch under the houses and past the Pizzeria al Mulino on the right. In a further 100m/yds, facing a large building with three arches, turn right up a narrow road. • After only 40m/yds, turn left up a long gentle flight of steps. This path now leads easily in 2km/1.3mi up the Valley of the Mills. On leaving the houses it becomes unpaved, but stone steps are in place for any steep stretches. The path winds through woods, with the stream on the left and passes three derelict mills within the woods. After an overgrown arch is seen on the left, the path rises up a short flight of steep steps. On the short level section that follows, turn sharp right by plaque number 13 (of a themed walk) and a sign, 'Sentiero Giustini Fortunato'. • After 200m/yds on the side path, pass above two small water supply buildings, then shortly fork left, to join a paved path. • Continue contouring gently upwards, passing the occasional house. More houses are reached. Some 1km/0.6mi from the valley, at a three-way junction where each path passes under an arch, go left to the square in Pontone (or head right downhill, following **Walk segment 6b** back to Amalfi).

12b Pontone to Amalfi
Time: 1h30min; *Grade:* easy

With your back to the Blu Bar in Pontone square, take the path straight ahead. It ascends a little and then descends. After 200m/yds, at a three way junction where each path passes under an arch, turn right. • Continue along this path past the occasional house, always contouring with the hillside up on your right. Beyond the last house, the well-paved path leads down to two small water supply buildings. Pass to the right of these buildings and descend on an earthen path gradually to the valley floor, where you meet the path running along the floor of the Valley of the Mills. • Turn left and follow the path past ruined mills and through woods back to Amalfi.

13 Minuta to Pogerola (Valle delle Ferriere)

This well-marked path takes you easily into the rugged hinterland of the Lattari Mountains. Although never more than a couple of miles as the crow flies from Amalfi, up here you are in a different world, amidst high pastures, remote woodlands, and magnificent mountains that rise to over 1200m/3700ft.; superb views abound. After a stiff initial climb, the route contours into the upper reaches of the Valle delle Ferriere and out again to Pogerola, always with the mountain slope up to your right. The path maintains a height roughly half-way between sea-level and the mountaintops. • Those unused to high-mountain walking should note that the path is rough underfoot and that occasionally you need a steadying hand on steeper sections. In a few places the path skirts very high, steep drops; you must be sure-footed and have a head for heights. The route is always easy to follow (even in mist), with good CAI red or red and white paint markings. You have to cross a stream on stones (not recommended if in spate). • If uncertain of your ability to tackle this route, you can get very good views of the valley by taking the short walk described in the footnote, which descends to Pontone. • If starting in Amalfi, consider taking the bus to Scala and walking up the road from there to the Minuta

The Valle delle Ferriere path (Walk segment 13)

hairpin bend where the walk starts, eliminating the climb to Minuta. **Photograph above**

Time: 3h40min; *Grade:* moderate, with a *height gain* of 150m/500ft

From the apex of the Minuta hairpin bend, take the steep flight of steps straight up the hillside. Follow this for about 300m/yds, to a prominent four-way junction. Here turn left along a level path marked with a horizontal red paint bar. [The short cut from Campidoglio comes in here.] • The path contours and rises gently for 400m/ yds until, on rounding a bend to the right, what is perhaps the outstanding viewpoint of the whole district is reached, known as Bosco Grande. You have a bird's-eye view of Amalfi, Atrani and Ravello. • The continuing path, now rough underfoot, enters a wood with a ➥. It then goes through a short tunnel* and contours high open mountainside, beside a water pipe, mostly buried, and some signs for a nature reserve. Red, then red and white CAI markings give frequent reassurance that you are on the correct route. • On reaching the main stream, cross at the first obvious spot and follow the CAI marks to the left, initially alongside the stream. (The stream has scoured interesting rock formations out of its bed at this point) • The path rises gently through woods for 700m/ yds to a side-stream crossing. After 100m/yds more, be alert to the main path turning sharp right, directly up the hillside. After a second stream crossing, the path rises gently (swathes of cyclamen in May and autumn) for 500m/yds to a prominent fork with faded CAI marks on trees. Keep left on the lower

*A much shorter version of this walk gives an excellent view of the Valle delle Ferriere before making a dramatic descent on a fine old path with splendid views down to Amalfi. *Time from the Minuta hairpin bend:* 1h30min; *Grade:* moderate with a *height gain* of 100m/330ft. After this tunnel, continue on the path, first bending right, then descending gradually in a broad curve to the left. Just after the entrance to a nature reserve, fork left and then bend sharply left again on a prominent mule track. This descends gradually to Pontone.

path by a fence. The path winds through abandoned terraces and then well-tended terraces, improving as it goes. At one point, it descends the bed of a stream which is usually dry. Eventually you enter Pogerola from the north.

14 Atrani — Pontone

This splendid segment follows the original path between the two villages.
Photograph page 47

14a Atrani (Piazza Umberto) to Atrani
Time: 1h; *Grade:* moderate, with *height gain* of 300m/1000ft

From the Piazza Umberto with its drinking fountain, take the road with the hoop-patterned paving straight up through Atrani. Just before it ends, by three palm trees on the right, take steep narrow steps up to the right. These bend left, running parallel with the valley floor, and lessen in gradient. Once you have left Atrani the steps cease and the path becomes a gently-ascending narrow road. Some 200m/yds after a zigzag, take a path going half-left down to the stream. Having crossed this, just before the gate to a house, go up right. This path now leads up to Pontone. On meeting houses turn right at a T-junction [**Walk segment 16** to Torre dello Ziro goes left here], and continue to the road. Cross this directly and shortly turn left into Pontone piazza.

14b Pontone to Atrani (Piazza Umberto)
Time: 45min; *Grade:* easy

Leave the square in Pontone by the arch to the left of the chapel. Turn right immediately down to the road. Cross diagonally and pass a chapel on the left, to descend gently by houses. After 150m/yds turn sharp left, still on steps [**Walk segment 16** to Torre dello Ziro goes straight on here] and descend below the houses. After about 250m/yds take a level path on a shelf (perhaps overgrown), going left — do not continue down very narrow steps onto a lemon terrace. The path is level for some 100m/yds, then it descends to a streamside. Follow this left to a bridge and up to a narrow road. Go right on this to Atrani, taking a downward path at junctions.

15 Atrani — Minori

This excellent segment is made up of three stretches: first, a dramatic ascent from Atrani on the Ravello path; next, a quiet stretch among lemon groves with fine coastal views; and finally, the descent from Torello on the Ravello to Minori route. **Photographs page 8 and opposite**

15a Atrani (Piazza Umberto) to Minori (Piazza Umberto)
Time: 1h45min; *Grade:* moderate, with a *height gain* of 230m/750ft

Take **Walk segment 3a** (page 41) as far as the house with the round windows. • From here follow the level path to the right. When you come to the main Ravello road, cross it diagonally and continue along the path on the far side. It contours past a couple of houses and then becomes earthen and passes through lemon groves. Some 500m/yds from the road, the path comes out onto a road that rises to the left. Go left for just 30m/yds, then take the steps that rise steeply to the left. (These steps may be overgrown with weeds at the outset; do not be discouraged.) • The steep steps rise for about 150m/yds; then the path bends to the right to resume contouring the hillside. It runs through lemon groves, rising gently. After 600m/0.35mi, you reach the houses of Torello. At the two T-junctions encountered, turn left. Soon you reach a chapel and the Ravello to Minori path: turn right and follow **Walk segment 5a** (page 44) from Torello down to Minori.

15b Minori (Piazza Umberto) — Atrani (Piazza Umberto)
Time: 1h45min; *Grade:* moderate, with a *height gain* of 230m/750ft

Take **Walk segment 5b** (page 45) from Minori to Torello. From the chapel in Torello, turn left down the Via Toretta Marmorata. After about 50m/yds, turn right in front of a house, down Via Vallone Casanova. After a further 200m/yds, turn right again. The path becomes earthen and contours the hillside. Ignore steps down to the left. After 600m/0.35mi the path descends steep steps to the left for 150m/yds, and you reach a road. Follow the road downhill for only 30m/yds, then take the short flight of steps up to the right and contour the hillside. Follow this path for 500m/yds, to the main Ravello road. Cross this diagonally and continue level for 200m/yds, to a T-junction by a house with round windows. Turn left here and continue down to Atrani via **Walk segment 3b**, page 43.

The descent to Santa Maria Maddalena in Atrani (Walk segments 3 and 15, Excursion 4)

16 Pontone to Torre dello Ziro

This walk should not be missed: it explores the spectacular promontory that separates Atrani from Amalfi, visits three superb viewpoints, and culminates in a visit to the castle that dominates both towns, the Torre dello Ziro. Here the unfortunate Queen Giovanna d'Aragona lived and was later beheaded. The whole promontory is an enchanting mix of limestone cliffs, pine woods, rockery plants and wild flowers. The paths are well built and are probably unique in the district — being built for leisure, unlike the older work-a-day routes. That is, unless they were built for executioners going about their business... Photographs page 44, 47 and below

Time: 1h round trip; *Grade:* easy, with a *height gain* of 100m/330ft

Leave the square in Pontone by the arch to the left of the chapel. Turn right immediately, down to the road. Cross diagonally to a chapel. The path continues gently down, past houses, to where the path turns sharp left. [**Walk segment 14** goes down here.] Go straight ahead along a narrow path at the edge of a terrace. [After about 50m/yds, the short-cut from Amalfi comes down stone steps from the right; see **Walk segment 6a** (Amalfi to Pontone), option ②.] • The concrete steps leading up to the start of the promontory can be seen ahead. Ascend these to a viewpoint, and then descend a little to a level stretch by a fanciful concrete structure. Three paths lead from here along the promontory. The path down to the left leads directly to the Torre dello Ziro along the left flank of the promontory; at one point, about half-way along, you must descend a number of zigzags. The path straight ahead leads to the second viewpoint. • For the best route, climb to the fourth terrace on the right. Follow this round to the right; it takes you to a wonderful broad flight of stone steps, seemingly suspended in space above Amalfi and the Valley of the Mills. Picnicking at the top of these steps, in sun or shade, is idyllic. Here, and at the second viewpoint 100m/yds further on, there are several

Looking down from the third viewpoint to the Torre dello Ziro and Atrani (Walk segment 16).

Descending from Ravello to Minori (Walk segment 17)

remains of a medieval defensive position. You can now descend to the path on the left; it leads to the third viewpoint — even more vertiginous than the second, but recently rebuilt in an ugly fashion. Retrace your steps a short way from this third viewpoint, and take the downhill path. It brings you quickly to the Torre dello Ziro path, just above the zigzags. • Return along the same paths — high cliffs bar progress in any other direction!

17 Ravello to Minori

In contrast to Walk segment 5 (the 'tourist' route between the two towns), this segment follows little-used paths, mostly past olive terraces. The views across the valley to San Nicola and the mountains beyond are always magnificent. Halfway down there is a perfect picnic site in front of a small chapel, or, if you are seeking shade, another possibility much lower down in a little piazza in the back streets of Minori. **Photograph above**

Time: 1h10m; *Grade:* easy, with a *descent* of 400m/1300ft

Follow **Walk segment 8a** (page 47) from Ravello through Lacco to Piazza Andrea Mansi and a chapel. Turn right in front of the chapel, down Via Famiglia d'Afflitto. Soon cross a road and continue ahead, descending for 200m/yds, to a junction where the level path goes ahead to an electricity pylon. • Do *not* go to the pylon; turn down right, after 100m/yds coming to the Casa Rossa. From this house keep to the left, descending steps or contouring, winding through olive groves. When you come to a T-junction with a splendid view of Minori, turn left and continue downhill. After about 200m/yds, a small chapel on the right, bounded by a low wall and seat, makes a lovely grassy picnic area. In late March we saw a bee orchid here. • A succession of steps and level stretches carries you to a slightly rising incline by a green railing. Beyond another level stretch, steps take you down to a T-junction: turn right, keeping to the main path. After another 250m/yds, still descending, now among houses, you come a prominent four-way junction. Turn right on Via Villa Amena, after 200m/yds coming to a shady piazza in front of two chapels, with ••► and seating. Continue to a motor road; cross half-left and go on to enter Minori at a T-junction of alleys. Turn right for the Roman villa and sea-front.

Positano/Praiano

Positano lies at the centre of the coastline that stretches from Colli di San Petro in the west, where the Amalfi Drive begins, to the deep cleft of Furore in the east. West of Positano the road runs on a shelf carved out of cliffs that rise sheer from the sea and soar up to the mountains above — a desolate, wild and uninhabited landscape. East of Positano the mountains rise to their highest anywhere on the coast, and hardly less steeply than in the west. But the villages of Monte Pertuso and Nocelle cling high on the hillsides, surrounded by terraces of vines and vegetables and separated by maybe the most profound chasm of them all, 350m/1000ft deep. Further east still the slopes relent a little behind the villages of Vèttica Maggiore and Praiano, to become steep and wild once more before reaching the gorge of Furore.

Apart from the two mountain segments (Nos. 26 and 30) the paths in this area are exceptionally well constructed. Steepness of terrain dictates that this network often consists of long flights of steps or zigzags, but they are mostly not too steep, offering perhaps the most exhilarating walking in the whole coastline — as the photographs in this section testify.

Getting About

Buses. Positano, Vèttica Maggiore and Praiano lie on the SITA route from Amalfi to Sorrento, which keeps to the main coast road all the way. As seen on the town plan, the coast road does not enter the central part of Positano, but keeps behind the town at a height of between 100m and 200m (350-700ft). From the centre of Positano, the easiest means of access to the coast road is to walk up the Via Cristoforo Colombo from the Piazza dei Mulini. (This is the internal bus terminus; buy your SITA tickets in the Bar Mulino Verde here.) Continue up to the coast road to the east of town; this is its lowest point, the Sponda bus stop. The other principal SITA stop, the Bar Internazionale (tickets available here, too), lies to the north — much higher up.

Two local bus services operate in Positano, leaving

KEY
road
Coast road
Minor road
Alley
Steps

0   200m/yds

Walk segment 19

Via Cristoforo Colombo

BEACH

POSITANO

to
Monte
Pertuso

FORNILLO

Via Pasitea

BEACH

Walk segment 24

Walk segment 25

1 Tourist office
2 Piazza dei Mulini
  (internal bus terminus)
3 Sponda bus stop
4 Bar Internazionale bus stop
5 Bivio Monte Pertuso bus stop
6 Post office
7 Ferries to Amalfi and Salerno
8 Ferries to Capri and Sorrento
9 Santa Maria Assunta (church)

from the Piazza dei Mulini. A town bus does an anti-clockwise circuit of the town at half-hourly or hourly intervals. It heads up the Via Cristoforo Colombo to the coast road at Sponda, follows the coast road to the Bar Internazionale, and then returns to the town centre on the one-way town road.

Another bus goes to Monte Pertuso and Nocelle (see timetable on page 131). Buy your tickets on board. If you are coming from another town and wish to connect with this bus, you can do so at various stops on the main coast road where it makes way behind and above Positano. Perhaps the obvious one is where the Monte Pertuso road leaves the coast road at the western end of Positano (the 'Bivio Monte Pertuso' bus stop).

Tourist Sights
Positano itself is the sight, colour-washed houses piled on the curving hillsides, topped by towering mountains. The area behind the Piaggia Grande and along the Via dei Mulini constitutes the centre, with its almost overpowering number of boutiques. Restaurants and bars are to be found in profusion. Around the corner to the west lies a much quieter part of town, Fornillo.

There are three fine churches in the area: Santa Maria Assunta, near the beach in Positano, San Gennaro in Vèttica Maggiore (see caption for the photograph on pages 72-73), and San Luca in Praiano.

Walk Planning Tips
The mountainside behind Positano and Praiano is the steepest of the whole coast. Walking here, usually on well-built paths among pines and cypress, with sensational coastal and mountain views, is utterly exhilarating. But if you're not careful, you will find yourself doing a lot of climbing. Good planning is the key. Use the bus up to Monte Pertuso or (from Amalfi) to Bomerano in Agerola, and start walking from there. A group based in Positano might hire a taxi to Bomerano.

The outstanding circuit in this area starts from Monte Pertuso: Walk segment 22a, followed by 23a and 24a. For easy walks, see Excursions 11 and 12.

From Monte Pertuso you can follow the Sentiero degli Dei (Walk segment 26b), and then take 27a for an easy return by bus from Vèttica to Positano. The Sentiero degli Dei can also be done by those staying in Amalfi: start from Bomerano and do Walk segments 28a, 26a, 20b and 19b.

The best of all the mountain routes is Walk segment 30, which starts from Colli di San Pietro.

WALK SEGMENTS

18 Positano circuit
This little circuit of Positano takes you to the quieter parts of Fornillo beach and town, and back through the centre of Positano. You will walk entirely by passageways and steps, meeting motor roads only to cross them. The climb up from Fornillo beach is quite sustained.

Time: 45min; *Grade:* moderate, with a *height gain* of 140m/460ft

From the west end of the main beach (the right-hand end, when you are looking out to sea), take the delightful coastal path (Via d'America) around the headland into a small valley. Ignore the tunnel and continue

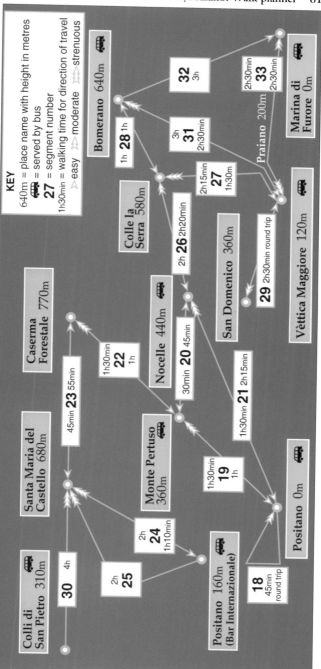

KEY

640m = place name with height in metres

🚌 = served by bus

27 = segment number

1h30min = walking time for direction of travel

➤ easy ➤➤ moderate ➤➤➤ strenuous

round to Fornillo beach. Follow paving slabs set in the sand past buildings on the right, to find steps leading up the hill. Ascend these until you reach Fornillo church. • Here keep right along a level path which takes you round to the right, into and out of a valley and up to a T-junction, where you turn right along a level path to a road. Go right along the road and then immediately turn left up steps (Via Maria Netti) to another road. Here turn right but, after 40m/yds, turn left along a narrow alley (Via dei Glicini). • On coming to a T-junction by a road, turn right and descend the path. After 100m/yds cross a road and descend (Via San Giovanni) to a tiny piazza in front of a chapel. Turn left or right here; both routes descend to the road again (➻ here). • Cross the road half-left and descend (Via degli Oleandri) a few zigzags to a T-junction. Turn left (signposted 'alla spiaggia'), to reach the centre of town again, behind the main beach.

19 Monte Pertuso — Positano

Monte Pertuso is a small quiet village perched in a commanding position on the mountainside 365m/1200ft above Positano. It takes its name from a crag above, pierced ('pertuso') by an enormous hole. The village is important to walkers because the local bus service from Positano gives effortless height gain to the start of some fine walks. In the village you will find a splendidly-situated old church (Santa Maria delle Grazie), a bar, restaurants and an excellent 'alimentari' for your picnic shopping. There are ➻s by the churchyard entrance and 50m/yds to the left of the 'alimentari'. **Photograph page 32**

19a Positano to Monte Pertuso
Time: 1h30min; *Grade:* strenuous, with a *height gain* of 360m/1180ft

From the main beach at Positano, ascend to the church; beyond it, go left up Via dei Mulini, towards the local bus terminus in the Piazza dei Mulini. About 100m/yds short of the bus terminus, turn sharp right up Via Leucosia; this takes you to a road (Via Cristoforo Colombo). Here turn right up the road. • After 100m/yds, look for steps ascending left. These lead after 150m/yds to the main coast road. Turn left for 20m/yds, then go right up a block-paved road by a SITA bus stop (also signposted 'Cimitero'). • Continue around the bend and the road becomes a path which you follow, always ascending, to Monte Pertuso. At a junction midway up the hillside, keep right.

19b Monte Pertuso to Positano
Time: 1h; *Grade:* easy, with a *descent* of 260m/850ft

Two descents are possible. ① From the main piazza on the 'mountain' side of the road in Monte Pertuso, take the path straight across the road, to pass to the right-hand side of the church. • This path winds downhill between houses, keeping left at a couple of junctions, to reach the hillside among terraces. The path descends, mostly through olive groves and down steps, to the upper houses of Positano and later a block-paved road. ② From the inner left-hand corner of the piazza take the alley going half-left. After 250m/yds of gentle ascent, go left down steps, cross the road, and continue down, turning right after just 10m/yds. Broad steps take you down to the first houses in Positano and a T-junction. Turn left and continue for 100m/yds, to a block-paved road. ➡ The block-paved road descends to the main coast road by a SITA stop (for buses to other towns). To reach the centre of Positano, go left for 20m/yds, then descend steps on the right.

20 Monte Pertuso — Nocelle

*Nocelle lies in a position on the mountainside equally as commanding as that occupied by Monte Pertuso, some 80m/250ft higher and 1km further east. It is separated from Monte Pertuso by a 350m/1000ft-deep chasm. Nocelle consists of just one delightful flower-filled alley contouring the hillside and a path leading down to its church (by a shrine and a ➡). The shrine offers shelter from rain, with seats. You can picnic here or in the piazza by the church. There is also a bar/restaurant with a dramatic view. The road and bus service has recently been extended from Monte Pertuso to Nocelle. **Photograph page 32***

20a Monte Pertuso to Nocelle
Time: 45min; *Grade:* easy, with a *height gain* of 60m/200ft

From the piazza in Monte Pertuso, turn left to ascend the road. Follow this for 1.5km/1mi and cross the ravine via an impressive arched bridge. • Just after the bridge, take a well-built concrete path on the right, which traverses the steep hillside to Nocelle. Once in Nocelle, you see the restaurant after 50m/yds and the central path junction with the shrine after 150m/yds.

20b Nocelle to Monte Pertuso
Time: 30min; *Grade:* easy

From the central path junction by the shrine in Nocelle, take the level concrete path. This leads through and out of the village and across a steep hillside, to the road. Follow the road down to Monte Pertuso.

21 Nocelle — Positano

Before the path from Monte Pertuso was built, in comparatively recent times, the main link to civilisation for the inhabitants of Nocelle was an imposing flight of steps directly down the mountainside to the main coast road. It is hardly surprising, therefore, that these steps are remarkably well constructed and easily graded, though they carry hardly any traffic nowadays. It's easy to do this walk by first taking the bus up to Nocelle. You have to be a bit of a masochist to ascend from the road to Nocelle, but some people do it just the same, so directions for walking up are given as well — Walk segment 21b.

21a Nocelle to Positano
Time: 1h30min; *Grade:* easy, with a *descent* of 340m/1120ft

From the central path junction by the shrine in Nocelle, take the steps down to the shady piazza in front of the small church, Santa Croce. From here steps lead down past the cemetery and out onto the wild hillside. The steps lead through light woodland redolent of rosemary, with dramatic glimpses of Positano, the coast and the mountainous backdrop. Half-way down there is a small cave containing a statuette of the Madonna, where you could shelter from rain. Near the coast road you pass some houses set in flower gardens. • On reaching the road turn right. [After just a few metres/yards, steps lead down to a public beach.] In the short space of 1km/0.6mi, this road takes you across three valleys, to the fork where Via Cristoforo Colombo leads down to the centre of Positano. At the second left-hand bend, notice the water trough donated by a Lady Banbury and maintained by the Italian League for the Protection of Animals. A ➟ here now provides water for human travellers.

21b Positano to Nocelle
Time: 2h15min; *Grade:* strenuous, with a *height gain* of 420m/1375ft

From the main beach take the alley past the church up to Piazza dei Mulini. Ascend to the coast road at the Sponda bus stop (see 'Getting about' on page 58. Turn right (towards Amalfi) and follow the road for 1km/0.6mi, around three right-hand bends. (At the second bend notice the water trough and ➟; see notes in **Walk segment 21a**). Beyond the third bend, look for steps ascending on the left, by a SITA stop (there is also a telephone kiosk below these steps). • Ascend the steps to Nocelle (see path description in **Walk segment 21a**.)

22 Monte Pertuso — Caserma Forestale
The steep mountainside behind Monte Pertuso, clad in the most aromatic of cypresses, pines, rosemary and myrtle, affords outstanding views along the coast and up into the highest of the Lattari Mountains. This segment gives access to a set of well-constructed paths crossing the mountainside. The

Right: An excellent path leads up high above Monte Pertuso to the Caserma Forestale (Walk segment 22). The dome of Monte Comune (Walk segment 30) can be seen in the distance.

Caserma (barracks) Forestale is a solid stone building with two grilled windows, nestling in the forest. The path has to gain a fair amount of height — hence the 'strenuous' grade — but it is not too steep and is in shade for much of the way. An optional extension is described to one of the outstanding viewpoints of the peninsula, 'I Trasiti', a superb picnic spot.
Photographs pages 32, 67 and below

22a Monte Pertuso to the Caserma Forestale

Time: 1h30min (for the detour to the Trasiti viewpoint, add 100m/ 330ft; 35min return); *Grade:* strenuous, with a *height gain* of 400m/1300ft

Take the road uphill from Monte Pertuso and go

150m/yds beyond the first right-hand bend, then climb left up steps by iron railings. (If travelling by bus, alight here, *one stop beyond* Monte Pertuso.) These steps, steep at first but gradually easing into a path as they rise, lead all the way to the Caserma Forestale. The path zigzags straight uphill for the first half of the climb and then goes mainly left. *Note: After perhaps an hour's climbing, keep level on the main path; ignore the steps rising to the right.* • From the Caserma Forestale, you can take a detour to the viewpoint shown opposite. To get there, take the zigzag path behind the Caserma for 100m/yds, then turn right on the lower of two tracks marked with red/white CAI waymarks. This track leads gradually up to the rocky shelf seen in the photograph opposite, after 20 minutes' walking from the Caserma. If you continue on the path you enter the most stupendous chasm on the peninsula, eventually reaching a point where the path was blocked by a massive rockfall in 2002. Return to the Caserma by the same route. One December we met two men here carrying baskets overflowing with *porcini* mushrooms.

22b Caserma Forestale to Monte Pertuso

Time: 1h; *Grade:* easy, with a *descent* of 400m/1300ft

Take the path going down from the Caserma Forestale, which leads down to the road above Monte Pertuso. The path goes mainly left across the slope in its first half and then zigzags straight down. Turn right on the road.

23 Caserma Forestale — Santa Maria del Castello

Santa Maria del Castello is a church sitting on a promontory high above Positano. There is a bar/restaurant nearby. Connecting the church to the Caserma lies a wonderfully-constructed balcony path that threads its way at an easy gradient between the pines, with the most stunning views down a wild cypress-studded mountainside to Positano. Confusingly, signs have been erected recently to label this as the 'Sentiero degli Dei', the name rightfully given to Walk segment 26. This is a walk to savour.

23a Caserma Forestale to Santa Maria del Castello

Time: 45min; *Grade:* easy

Looking down the hillside at the Caserma Forestale, take the well-built path to the right; initially it rises gently. It is joined shortly by another path and starts a gently descending traverse across the mountainside lasting 2km/1.2mi. On emerging from the forest, the path threads through some smallholdings, to reach a road. Turn left and walk 400m/yds to the church.

23b Santa Maria del Castello to the Caserma Forestale

Time: 55min; *Grade:* easy, with a *height gain* of 90m/300ft

Walk segment 22a (detour): From this rock ledge, 'I Trasiti', your views stretch past Monte Comune (Walk segment 30) along the coast as far as Capri, with Ischia off to the right. Nocelle lies below, and Positano is seen on the coast. Even if you have little walking experience, the beautifully-constructed paths will, on a fine day, lead you here safely.

From the church drive turn right along the road for 400m/yds. Turn right again, on a rough concrete road through some smallholdings. After about 100m/yds, as it enters the forest, this becomes a well-built path, which now traverses the mountainside, gently ascending. After 2km/1.2mi, a prominent fork is reached: go right on the gently descending path for about 100m/yds to the solid stone building of the Caserma Forestale. Now consider making a detour to the Trasiti viewpoint shown above (see **Walk segment 22a**).

24 Santa Maria del Castello — Positano

This well-graded ancient paved path provides a sensational yet easy return from the heights of Santa Maria del Castello to the fleshpots of Positano. Zigzagging down, you see the roofs of the town and the beach as in an aerial photograph, with extensive panoramas left to the Lattari mountain range. You might consider making the ascent if it's not too hot; I once met a middle-aged woman, obviously a local, climbing slowly in her underclothes, black dress neatly folded over an arm. I scarcely think she expected to meet anyone that evening. Although rated strenuous on account of the height difference, the path is not too steep and has few steps.
Photograph pages 68-69

24a Santa Maria del Castello to Positano (Bar Internazionale)
Time: 1h10min; *Grade:* easy, with a *descent* of 520m/1700ft
Leaving the church drive, turn left. In 200m/yds you come to a crossing of minor roads: turn left. The narrow tarmac road turns right after 50m/yds: here continue

straight ahead on a field path. Once at the edge of the plateau, go left for 100m/yds, to find the start of the paved path down to Positano. • The path descends a wild mountainside, finally reaching the upper houses of Positano and the Monte Pertuso road. Cross straight over the road and descend to a small piazza by the Chiesa Nuova. Follow the path round the right-hand side of the church to its rear, and descend to the main coast road by the Bar Internazionale (SITA stop and tickets; refreshments).

24b Positano (Bar Internazionale) to Santa Maria del Castello

Time: 2h; *Grade:* strenuous, with a *height gain* of 520m/1700ft

From the Bar Internazionale take Via Chiesa Nuova; it ascends straight up from the junction at the bend in the coast road. Beyond the church, steps take you up to the Monte Pertuso road. Go straight across, to join the path that climbs the mountainside. About one-third of the way up, ignore a minor path straight ahead; the main path turns sharp right. • At the top of the path, turn sharp left to contour on a field path just below the rim of the plateau. After only 100m/yds, take a path going right. After another 100m/yds, this leads you to a minor crossroads. Turn right here and reach the church of Santa Maria del Castello after a further 200m/yds.

25 Positano — Santa Maria del Castello

If wishing to ascend from the Bar Internazionale to Santa Maria del Castello on a hot day, you can take this segment as a shady alternative to the full sun of Walk segment 24. After a steep start it is generally less steep, too. It takes a now little-used but excellently-built path on the forest-clad slopes to the northwest of Positano. (In its

This ancient paved path snakes down the hillside from Santa Maria del Castello to Positano (Walk segment 24). Besides admiring the panoramic views you will feast your eyes on the orchids, rosemary, broom and many other flowers beside the path. The view on pages 28-29 is taken from further left, just below Santa Maria del Castello.

upper reaches, the path becomes rougher, and it is preferable to wear walking boots.) As you gain height, first glimpses and then full views of the coast and mountains are revealed. In May you will see many orchids. Only the ascent is described, as Walk segment 24, with its tremendous views, offers the obvious way down.

Time: 2h; *Grade*: strenuous, with a *height gain* of 530m/1740ft

From the Bar Internazionale walk west along the coast road for 300m/yds, to the Monte Pertuso turn-off. After just 30m/yds more, take the steep flight of steps, currently signposted 'Itinerario 1'. These zigzag, but soon the gradient relents, and an excellent path ascends the left-hand side of the valley, into the mountains. On coming to an isolated house (**25min**), pass to the left of it, to regain your stepped path. Before long this makes some zigzags up to a prominent turning sharp right (**45min**), ignoring the smaller path going straight ahead. For a short while there are red paint waymarks.

• From here the path will climb steadily to the summit, always with the slope up to the left (apart from some minor zigzags). Some 500m/yds along this path (**1h15min**), ignore the broad level path heading right; fork left, to ascend. After another 100m/yds (**1h22min**), at another fork, ignore the path on the left (alongside a barbed-wire fence); keep right on the lower, smaller path (a small stretch of which is in poor

Vineyards cling to the hillsides below the 'path of the Gods' (Sentiero degli Dei; Walk segment 26).

condition). On reaching easier grassy slopes, the path turns inland and joins the end of a narrow road. Walk on this past a house, and then go left around the bend, to a minor crossroads. Turn right and continue for 200m/yds to Santa Maria del Castello.

26 Colle la Serra — Nocelle

The wild mountainside east of Nocelle can be traversed along a popular but rough path that offers magnificent views of the mountains and coast, and lives up to its billing as the 'path of the Gods' (Sentiero degli Dei). Typically this segment will form part of a route from Bomerano to Positano (for walkers coming from Amalfi), or from Monte Pertuso to Vettica Maggiore (for those starting in Positano). **Photographs above, opposite, cover**

26a Colle la Serra to Nocelle
Time: 2h; *Grade:* easy

From the T-junction of mule tracks walk to the large garden (mesh fence, crucifix inside) and turn right. Descend steps for 100m/yds to a T-junction; here turn right (photograph opposite). Now walking parallel to the coast, pass a house and descend a rocky section to a junction [the path from **Walk segment 29** joins here]. Continue up onto a section with exhilarating views to the foot of a large cliff. The path now rises obliquely over some rocks to join a major path that leads to Nocelle, entering on a level path by houses. This turns sharp left down a few steps, to a path junction in the centre of the village, where you will find a shrine and ➡.

26b Nocelle to Colle la Serra
Time: 2h20min; *Grade:* moderate, with a *height gain* of 140m/460ft
From the path junction by the shrine in the centre of

Nocelle, climb the steps, soon turning right and heading out of the village. You will follow this well-used path for the next two hours, as you make way across the wild mountainside, either on the level or with a gently ascending tendency, and always with the slope up to your left. Any descents will be short-lived. • As you near the col (la Serra), you will see a few terraces and the path will lead you to a T-junction of wide mule tracks on a level stretch of path by a large garden (mesh fence, crucifix inside).

27 Colle la Serra — Vèttica Maggiore (or Praiano)

*Rough-hewn but solid steps and terraces lead from the col down to the coast towns, traversing a lonely, wild, beautiful hillside that was once quite intensively cultivated. Views west extend to Positano and the coast as far as Capri, while in the middle of the walk you get a good view of the monastery of San Domenico (Walk segment 29). • At the lower end of the path proper, but still some way above the towns, there is an outstanding viewpoint from where, on a clear day, you would be able to look along the whole coastline from Capri to Salerno. This could form the objective of a shortish walk for someone staying in one of the two villages — take the first part of Walk segment 27b. See notes on Vèttica in the caption for the **photograph on pages 72-73**.*

27a Colle la Serra to Vèttica Maggiore (and Praiano)

Time: 1h30min; *Grade:* easy, with a *descent* of 400m/1300ft

From the T-junction of mule tracks walk to the large garden (mesh fence, crucifix inside) and turn right. Descend steps for 100m/yds to a T-junction; here turn left (photograph below). At a junction (with ↦) 300m/yds further on, go straight ahead. Continue to descend steps, always with the slope up to the left. At times the path follows the edges of terraces. After about 1km/

Go right for the Sentiero degli Dei and left to descend to Praiano (Walk segments 26 and 27). San Domenico lies below.

0.6mi, the path passes a water supply building and then rounds the crest of the ridge, turning to the left. This is a splendid viewpoint. • Some 150m/yds further on, now on the eastern side of the ridge, turn right down a steep flight of steps (passing through an arch in a house), down to a road. • Cross the road and descend more steps, to a horizontal alley with staggered crossing of paths, with Via Oratorio descending to Praiano's church. [Here **Walk segment 31a** goes left and **segment 33a** takes Via Oratorio.] To continue to Vèttica, turn right along the horizontal alley. After 300m/yds you come to a superb viewpoint in front of a small chapel. • Just beyond the chapel, descend the concrete steps and turn left at the bottom, down to a road. Turn left and immediately right, to a lower road. This road narrows into an alley, descending gently between houses. After 200m/yds along the alley, you can turn left opposite a ↦, down to the main coast road near the centre of Vèttica. Or take the next left, for a more pleasant, if slightly longer, way down.

27b Vèttica Maggiore (or Praiano) to Colle la Serra

Time: 2h15min; *Grade:* strenuous, with a *height gain* of 460m/1500ft

Starting from the main coast road just above Vèttica church, in the small piazza (G Gagliano) with a fountain, climb the steps (Via F Russo). After 40m/yds turn left into an alley that takes you by easy stages up to a T-junction with a horizontal alley. Turn right here,

soon passing a ↦. • This alley rises gently between houses for 200m/yds and then breaks out onto a road. Shortly, turn left on another road, then immediately right up steps, soon turning right and ascending to a small chapel — from where there is a splendid view. • Take the path to the right of the chapel; it descends a little and, after 300m/yds, reaches a staggered crossing of paths, with Via Oratorio descending to Praiano's church. [**Walk segment 31a** continues ahead here; **segment 33a** descends Via Oratorio.] • Turn left up steps to cross a road and continue steeply up, passing through an arch under a house, and going round a bend to the left. In a further 150m/yds, where the path moves over to the west side of the ridge, you will reach the splendid viewpoint mentioned in the introduction to this segment. • The path now ascends on steps, interspersed with level stretches along the edges of terraces. The hillside is always up to your right. At a couple of junctions near the top of the climb (↦ at one of them), keep ahead up steps. You will know you have reached the Colle la Serra: there is a T-junction of wide mule tracks by a large garden (mesh fence, crucifix inside).

28 Bomerano — Colle la Serra

Easy walking across a steep rugged hillside connects Bomerano with the Sentiero degli Dei which leads to Nocelle (Walk segment 26), or Walk

segment 27 down to Vèttica/ Praiano. En route you pass under the cave of Grotta Biscotta, which is reputed to contain medieval animal

Looking west across Vèttica Maggiore to Positano and the coastline as far as Capri (Walk segments 27, 29, 31 and 33). The domes of the church of San Gennaro glisten in early morning sunlight. This church, and its wide piazza just below the road, are well worth a visit. The bronze doors consist of fourteen finely-cast panels depicting San Gennaro's life story, and nearby there are bronze busts of Matthew, Mark, Luke and John. There is a tap in an alley just below the church and the path to the beach begins here.

pens. • The Agerola bus from Amalfi takes a most sensational route. The road gains height consistently in a series of bends and tunnels that follow the contours of the terrain, threading through communities clinging to the mountainside. After passing into and out of the deep valley of Furore, the road starts on a series of serpentine bends through the village of Furore, noted for its artists' colony and for fine wine, to arrive finally at the 600m/2000ft-high plain of Agerola. Spare a thought for the cyclists of the Tour of Italy, who must sometimes make this climb — at the summit there is a monument to the legendary Italian cyclist Fausto Coppi. • After the road has levelled off and turned inland for 1km, it bends right and then left. Your bus stop comes after 0.5km more. Take the narrow road left by the no entry sign to reach Bomerano town centre, where you will find a ⟶.

28a Bomerano to Colle la Serra
Time: 1h; *Grade:* easy

Facing the large church in Bomerano, take the narrow road going left out of the square (Via Pennino; numerous walking signs including 'Sentiero degli Dei'). The road, with crazy paving, descends, passes under a road bridge and, after 250m/yds, goes down a few steps. Turn right and head for some rough concrete steps. • On reaching the road, turn left. Follow the road to its end in 500m/yds, where it descends below the Grotta Biscotta and becomes a mule track (⟶). Enjoying wide views down to the left, follow the track for 1km/0.6mi to the Colle la Serra — a T-junction of wide mule tracks by a large garden (mesh fence, crucifix inside).

28b Colle la Serra to Bomerano
Time: 1h; *Grade:* easy, with a *height gain* of 60m/200ft

With your back to the large garden (mesh fence, crucifix inside), take the wide mule track going half-right. This mostly-level path traverses the hillside, with wide views down to the right. After 1km/0.6mi you reach broad concrete steps (⟶) below the Grotta Biscotta. The steps merge with a road, which you follow for 500m/yds, watching for rough narrow concrete steps going down to the right. • Descend these steps. Join a track which ascends to the left. Follow this for 250m/yds up to the main piazza of Bomerano. The SITA bus to Amalfi stops here.

29 Vèttica Maggiore — San Domenico

The monastery of San Domenico lies on a rocky promontory high above the coast, overlooking Vèttica and Positano. Our excellent path passes the Fourteen Stations of the Cross as it ascends. The monastery, now abandoned, is still open. It is barely furnished but has pleasant, old, if somewhat damaged frescoes. Outside, a shady patio with ⟶ commands outstanding views down to Positano and along the coast — a splendid picnic spot. The path lies largely in shade before noon. A rocky path with superb

Terraced hillside above Marina di Furore (Walk segments 32 and 33)

views connects the monastery with the Sentiero degli Dei. **Photographs pages 2, 71, 72-73**

Time: 2h30min there and back; *Grade:* moderate, with a *height gain* of 230m/750ft

Starting from the main coast road just above Vèttica church, in the small piazza (G Gagliano) with a fountain, climb the steps (Via F Russo). After 40m/yds turn left into an alley that takes you by easy stages up to a T-junction with a horizontal alley. Turn left here. After about 100m/yds the path goes up gentle steps between houses, until it finally rounds a corner beyond the last house, and San Domenico comes into view high up on the hillside (↦ here). • After a short level section, take the well-built steps signposted to San Domenico; these lead past the 14 Stations of the Cross up to the monastery. [Just below the monastery piazza, a narrow path is signed 'Nocelle/Bomerano'. This ascends steeply to join **Walk segment 26a**.] • Return the same way, noting the following options. ① To descend quickly to the coast road, take the first right turn after the first level section among the houses. ② To extend the walk along the coast through Praiano and come down to the coast road further east, once among the houses, continue east along the alley. From here use the notes for **Walk segments 27b and 33a** to walk through Praiano.

30 Colli di San Pietro to Santa Maria del Castello

This walk, along the spine of mountains high above the corniche road to Positano from Sorrento, yields the most exhilarating of views along

the peninsula to Capri. There is a heightened sense of drama as the view changes once Monte Comune, the highest point, is reached. Suddenly a panorama opens of the wild mountainside sweeping down from the highest of the Lattari mountains to a bird's-eye view over Positano. This is a hike for well-shod confident walkers. The going is very rough in a few places, and there are no convenient escape routes. On reaching Santa Maria del Castello, you can quickly drop down by the delightful Walk segment 24 to Positano for buses and boats. **Photograph below**

Time: 4 hours; *Grade:* strenuous, with a *height gain* of 660m/ 2150ft

At the Colli di San Pietro crossroads (coming from the direction of Sorrento), turn left up Via S Pietro. Shortly pass a plaque to Robert Browning and continue for 300m/yds, to enter gates facing you. Walk up the drive and, after 50m/yds, turn right onto a path and go through the grounds of a villa, keeping to the right, to a crossroads above the estate. Turn sharp right onto a gravel track. After 100m/yds, by a red/white CAI waymark, continue ahead on an old path. This leads up the hillside in long gentle zigzags. After the fifth bend, the path heads up for 300m/yds, to the crest of the ridge. • Turn right onto a path descending obliquely on the other side. Your route up the rocky ridge to the dome of Monte Comune is now revealed. Descend to cross a meadow on the rim of the sea-cliff. Some

50m/yds before the path enters woods, turn right onto an indistinct path that leads to a better path running 30m/yds from the rim of the cliffs. Follow this path along the edge of the cliff, first up and then down to a col by two stone gate posts. • Continue along the ridge on a stony path for 50m/yds and, just *before* two CAI marks, transfer to the right-hand side of the ridge. Here you pick up a well-trodden path that ascends gradually, skirts the foot of large cliffs to the left, and zigzags up to the ridge again. Pick up more CAI marks to ascend along the crest, skirting to the left of a large cliff ahead. The path ascends to old terraces and then to the ruined building shown below. Past the building, ignore a new track going left, but instead continue ahead up the final rocky hillside, tending to the right and following occasional CAI marks. • At the top, go through a gap in the fence (possibly gated) on a path, now on the rim of Monte Comune, and continue until the path ends. Keep on in the same direction, on the edge of the flat summit of Monte Comune, following the line of a stout fence on your left for some 300m/yds. Then descend through another gated gap. Leaving the fence, take a narrow path with good CAI marking. After about 300m/yds, watch for the path turning left, to transfer to the next ridge.

Follow the CAI marks down a rocky stretch to a stout wooden fence. • Turn right, to follow the fence and carry on beyond it for 700m/yds, until you reach a paved road by two buildings. Just past these the road bends left. Here either turn right on Walk segment 24a to Positano, or turn left, then right, for Santa Maria del Castello (and the bar 'Zi Pepe').

Walk segment 30 takes us along the spine of Monte Comune where, from the 'part-ruined building', we look down on Sorrento in the distance.

31 Vèttica Maggiore — Bomerano

An excellent mule track, followed by a good path, leads delightfully up the west side of the Vallone di Praia, where you end up walking under large cliffs just before reaching Bomerano. Views are splendid and the walking a good mix of woodland and open path. **Photograph pages 72-73**

31a Vèttica Maggiore to Bomerano
Time: 3h; *Grade:* strenuous, with a *height gain* of 540m/1750ft

Follow **Walk segment 27b** as far as the staggered crossroads of paths above Praiano church. • Continue along the horizontal alley for another 500m, until it bends left into a large valley and becomes unsurfaced. Now follow this mule track up the left hand side of the valley, ascending gradually, for about 1km. • You then fork left onto a well-built flight of steps heading towards a large yellow cliff towering above. This path, initially on wide rough steps and later much narrower and threading through vegetation, ascends rather more steeply and curves gradually to the right. • Nearing the cliffs above, at a T-junction with another well-established path, turn left and follow this up to Bomerano. [**Walk segment 32** goes right at this junction.] On passing directly by the foot of the large cliff, be alert to the signposted Grotta di Dilappi.

31b Bomerano — Vèttica Maggiore
Time: 2h30min; *Grade:* easy, with a *descent* of 540m/1750ft

Facing the large church in Bomerano, take the narrow crazy-paved Via Pennino going left out of the square (various walking signs mark the start). Descend this road, go under a bridge and then down steps to join an earthen path, always keeping straight ahead. Soon the view down to the coast opens up and the path descends left on broken steps. On passing directly by the foot of a large cliff, be alert to the signposted Grotta di Dilappi. • 100m further on, at a junction of paths, fork right down a flight of steps. [**Walk segment 32** continues ahead here.] At the foot of the steps the path turns sharp right. Continue on the path, descending the hillside, with the slope up to your right, making a broad curve to the left. Initially the path is narrow, threading through vegetation, and later it descends broad rough steps. These lead to a level mule track. • Turn right and follow the track, descending the right-hand side of the valley for about 1km, until the path becomes surfaced and bends right into

Praiano. Walk another 500m to a staggered cross-roads of paths, where Via Oratorio descends to Praiano church. Follow **Walk segment 27a** to Vèttica Maggiore.

32 Bomerano to Marina di Furore

Bus passengers whizzing along the coast get a subliminal glimpse of the Furore 'fjord' as they cross the bridge over a chasm before plunging into the next tunnel. Although some buildings and a bit of beach can be seen, they have no chance to work out what the place is really like. Marina di Furore is the harbour that once served the hillside village of Furore and has recently been done up as a themed centre. On the way down from Bomerano the route descends a wild hillside under great cliffs; passes by the chapel of Sant'Alfonso di Liguori, an idyllic picnic spot; and passes through the little village of Sant'Elia. Much of the descent is on well-built steps. See Walk segment 28 for notes on buses to Bomerano. **Photograph page 75**

Time: 3h; *Grade:* easy, with a *descent* of 600m/2000ft

Follow **Walk segment 31b** to the junction just after the Grotta di Dilappi. • Continue ahead to a small col between the mountain on the left and a small rocky knoll. Here join a concrete path at a bend. Continue down and left to an asphalt road. [The path down to Sant'Alfonso leaves by steps from here, a 5min detour.] • Walk up the road for 250m/yds and, just beyond the first house, take steps down right through an arch to the main road. A few steps cut off the hairpin bend; beyond this a long flight of steps zigzags down a wild hillside to a minor road. Cross this and descend on yet more steps to the road at Sant'Elia. [Go right to the chapel and viewpoint. **Walk segment 33b** continues past these to Vèttica.] • Continue on steps opposite for the final descent down a wild hillside to the marina and the main coast road and bus stop. • Those wishing to connect with **Walk segment 36** in Conca dei Marini can take the path from the far (Amalfi) side of the bridge over the gorge. It follows the right-hand side of the gorge for 25 minutes, before rising by stone steps out of the gorge (20 minutes more). The path ends by the shrine at a bend in the road — see **Walk segment 36**.

33 Vèttica Maggiore — Marina di Furore

This segment contours through Praiano, past its church of San Luca; traverses a wild hillside to Sant'Elia on a well-marked if narrow and at times rocky path requiring an occasional helping hand; and then descends on good steps to Marina di Furore (see Walk segment 32 for a description of this). **Photographs pages 72-73 and 75**

33a Vèttica Maggiore to Marina di Furore

Time: 2h30min; *Grade:* moderate, with *height gain* of 150m/ 490ft

Follow **Walk segment 27b** as far as the staggered crossroads of paths above Praiano church. Take Via Oratorio down to the piazza by the church. • Continue between the church and its campanile. This path contours the coast, descending gradually, at one point going under a ceramic mural, until you reach the small Piazza Moressa: continue ahead on a level path for 300m/yds to a signposted fork. [Descend right to the coast road and the Marina di Praia for bars and a sea-level walkway.] • Fork left for the hillside path to Sant'Elia. This climbs steadily for 400m/yds, to pass under an untidy house and run into a side valley. Turn sharp right to resume the climb along the coast to Sant'Elia, just over 1km further on. • 100m/yds beyond the chapel, turn right down steps for the final descent down a wild hillside to the marina and the main coast road and bus stop. See note in **Walk segment 32** for extending the walk to Conca.

33b Marina di Furore to Vèttica Maggiore

Time: 2h30min; *Grade:* strenuous, with *height gain* of 250m/ 800ft

From the Praiano end of the road bridge over the gorge, walk inland to the start of the steps that lead up to Sant'Elia. After a 500m/yds climb, arrive at a road and turn left for the church and, beyond this, a viewpoint. • Now join the path to Praiano. This takes a gradually descending route parallel to the coast for 1km, running into a side valley. Turn sharp left here, to resume the path's descent, initally climbing to pass to the left of a house and then descending steeply for 400m/yds to the houses of Praiano, at a junction just as the paved alley starts. [Descend sharp left to the coast road and the Marina di Praia for bars and a sea-level walkway.] • Continue ahead on the level path for 300m/yds to the small Piazza Moressa. Take the alley half-right out of the piazza, and climb gently up to the church of San Luca and its piazza. • From the piazza ascend Via Oratorio to the path above at a staggered crossing of footpaths. Follow **Walk segment 27a** to Vèttica Maggiore.

Conca dei Marini

This small area covers the hillside between the coast at Conca and the lip of the Agerola Plain at San Lazzaro; it is bounded on the west by the chasm of Furore and on the east by the chapel of Lone.

Getting about

Buses. The coast road is served by the Amalfi/Sorrento route. The Amalfi/Agerola route serves San Lazzaro and, on the way up, passes Vèttica Minore and the former convent of Santa Rosa. Tovere is served infrequently by a direct bus from Amalfi.

The coast east to Amalfi, seen from a small piazza in Conca dei Marini (Walk segments 36 and 37; Excursion 10)

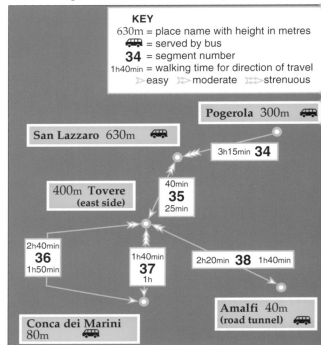

KEY
630m = place name with height in metres
🚐 = served by bus
34 = segment number
1h40min = walking time for direction of travel
▷ easy ▷▷ moderate ▷▷▷ strenuous

Pogerola 300m 🚐

San Lazzaro 630m 🚐

3h15min **34**

400m Tovere
(east side)

40min
35
25min

2h40min
36
1h50min

1h40min
37
1h

2h20min **38** 1h40min

Amalfi 40m
(road tunnel) 🚐

Conca dei Marini
80m 🚐

Tourist sight
The church of San Pancrazio at Conca and its view-point.

Walk planning tips
The best circuit of all involves taking the splendid Walk segment 34 from Pogerola to San Lazzaro in Agerola, and returning from there to Amalfi either by bus or by the old way used before motor roads were built, a lovely route, Walk segments 35a and 38b. An easy way to access the Conca dei Marini hillside is to take the bus to San Lazzaro (check the timetables as not all Agerola buses go all the way there). It's then downhill all the way by Walk segment 35a, followed by 36a or 37a.

WALK SEGMENTS

34 Pogerola to San Lazzaro
Excellent paths lead high into the mountains and down to San Lazzaro. The route sustains high interest and commanding views into the mountains and, later, along the coast, from quiet forest paths. The strenuous ascent on rough paths comes at the beginning of the Walk segment; once

this is over, although further height is gained gradually, it's a delightful easy stroll.

Time: 3h 15min; *Grade:* strenuous, with a *height gain:* 550m/1800ft

In Pogerola take the minor road opposite the drinking fountain. After 100m/yds take steps up left, then left again. These regain the road under a large modern building. Go left for 50m/yds to a hairpin bend, then go straight ahead on an asphalt track. After 100m/yds take steps up to the right of a block of flats. After 200m/yds of gentle ascent the path bends left under a small cliff and rounds a bend, coming to an old building with vines. Opposite the building, turn right up a rough rock ledge, to join a stony mule track. This continues in zigzags to the foot of the large cliff high above. (At a fork about 200m from the building, choose the left path along an eroded gully.) • At the foot of the cliff, at a ruined building, the path continues right, hugging the foot of the cliff. After 150m/yds you round a bend to the left. (Adventurous souls can go right just *before* the bend, taking narrow steps to a wonderful viewpoint.) • From the bend, you now want to keep left, rounding the Monte Molignano on three sides. After about 150m/ yds, fork left up to the foot of a cliff. After 250m/yds more you join a wide path coming up from the right, and shortly arrive at a spring (Acquolella), where water flows into a stone trough. From here the path has red/white CAI marks. Go up the rocky gully; at its top reach a broad path which climbs gently to the next corner of the mountain, where you curve right. • The broad path now rounds (to the left) three sides of a wide valley — at first level, then gently down, and finally climbing gently up the far side. After 250m/yds of this climb, where the path bends very sharply right, the route leaves the CAI marks

High above the coast, on the way to San Lazzaro (Walk segment 34)

Great bushes of tree-spurge (Euphorbia dendroides) *light up many walks. These can grow up to 2m/6ft in height.*

and climbs straight ahead, now following yellow marks on a rocky path for 150m/yds to a fine viewpoint and the end of a gravel road. After some 40m/yds on the road, turn left onto a narrow path parallel with the coast, which shortly joins a wider path. Follow this over the hill with pylons ahead, and down to San Lazzaro.

35 San Lazzaro — Tovere (east side)
This short segment connects San Lazzaro to an important path junction on the hillside on the east side of Tovere.

35a San Lazzaro to Tovere (east side)
Time: 25min; *Grade:* easy, with a *descent* of 230m/750ft
From the main square in San Lazzaro take the road down to the edge of the plateau. Just as the road bends right, steps descend left. Follow these downhill through open countryside for 300m/yds, to a path junction. Turn left and continue downhill, behind a couple of houses and past a pylon, from where there are fine views left along the coast to Amalfi. You reach a path junction by a cube-shaped concrete water supply building.

35b Tovere (east side) to San Lazzaro
Time: 40min; *Grade:* moderate, with a *height gain* of 200m/660ft
From the junction by the water supply building ascend the steps, past a pylon (fine views right along the coast to Amalfi) and a couple of houses. Some 500m/yds from the start, turn right at a junction, to ascend steps to San Lazzaro.

36 Tovere (east side) — Conca dei Marini
This segment wanders pleasantly across the hillside above Conca, as far as the rim of the deep ravine of Furore to the west; it then returns to Conca on a lower path. A connection is described to link to Marina di Furore (Walk segment 33). **Photograph page 81**

36a Tovere (east side) to Conca dei Marini
Time: 1h50min; *Grade:* easy, with a *descent* of 200m/660ft

From the path junction by the concrete water supply building, take the narrow road which ascends gradually. After some 400m/yds pass a small chapel and a ↟. [**Walk segment 37a** descends steps here.]

Shortly, at a wide road, turn left. • Follow this road, with little traffic, past a church on the right, counting the 14 Stations of the Cross beside the road. Three hairpin bends take you down to the Amalfi/Agerola road: turn left. • After 200m/yds, on a left-hand bend, take steps down to the right (between two houses, Nos 63 and 65). Descend on steps through light woodland. At the foot of the steps make your way down to the road below and turn right. [At the bend, by a covered shrine with seats, stone steps mark the start of the path down to Marina di Furore and **Walk segment 33**.] Continue down the road for about 600m/yds, to the church of San Antonio on the right. Turn right onto the path beside the church for some wonderful coastal views; after 200m/yds you rejoin the road. Some 200m/yds further on, take steps down to the right. These lead down to a fine view of the coast towards Amalfi and then to the church of San Pancrazio, with its commanding viewpoint to the west. • From the viewpoint, take the road, then use the path on the right to descend 150m/yds down to the coast road at Conca, by the Hotel Belvedere. (In summer, when the hotel is open, the Reception sells SITA tickets.)

36b Conca dei Marini to Tovere (east side)

Time: 2h40min; *Grade:* moderate, with a *height gain* of 320m/1050ft

From the Hotel Belvedere on the coast road at Conca, climb steps, and then a minor road, for 150m/yds, up to the church of San Pancrazio and its commanding viewpoint to the west. • From the upper side of the church (••), take gentle steps up to a minor road, where you continue to the right, up to a viewpoint to the east. Continue up steps for some 200m/yds to a minor road and turn left. [**Walk segment 37b** continues up steps here.] After 200m/yds take a few steps down left, to a stretch of level path (wonderful coast views) and the church of San Antonio. • Rejoin the road for some 600m/yds, going out of the village and up to a sharp bend by a covered shrine with seats. [Here stone steps mark the start of the path down to Marina di Furore and **Walk segment 33**.] Continue on the road for another 50m/yds and then make your way up over a bit of rough ground, to stone steps leading up the hillside to the main Amalfi/Agerola road. Turn left here. • After 200m/yds turn right up the Tovere road and follow it past three hairpin bends, the 14 Stations of the Cross, and a church on the left. Go

400m/yds past the church, then take a very narrow level road off to the right. Follow this for 500m/0.35mi, to its end at a path junction with a cube-shaped concrete water supply building on the left.

37 Tovere (east side) — Conca dei Marini

More direct than segment 36, this route goes past the prominently-sited former convent of Santa Rosa, now an hotel. **Photograph page 81**

37a Tovere (east side) to Conca dei Marini

Time: 1h; *Grade:* easy, with a *descent* of 320m/1050ft

Follow **Walk segment 36a** to the ➤➤ on the left; here take steps downhill. • At the foot of the steps go half-left and make for an iron gate in a wall, and then descend to an isolated old pylon. Here go left along a level field path. After going down a few steps, keep left on the level path, After another 300m/yds, at old houses, steps start and then turn downhill to the old Santa Rosa building. • Cross the road by the road tunnel and take the minor road signposted to Conca. Follow this for 500m/yds; just after you pass a high cliff on the right, take steps down to the left. • The steps level out by a fine viewpoint to the east, at a minor road. Follow the road for 50m/yds, then descend a final flight of steps to the church of San Pancrazio with its commanding viewpoint to the west. • From the viewpoint, take the road, then use the path on the right to descend 150m/yds down to the coast road at Conca, by the Hotel Belvedere. (In summer, when the hotel is open, the Reception sells SITA tickets.)

37b Conca dei Marini to Tovere (east side)

Time: 1h40min; *Grade:* strenuous, with a *height gain* of 320m/1050ft

Follow **Walk segment 36b** (page 85) past the viewpoint to the east and up steps to the road, where that segment turns left. Continue up steps to a higher road and there turn right. After 500m/yds you come to the old convent of Santa Rosa, now an hotel. Cross the road just by the road tunnel and take the steps that lead up above the tunnel. Then continue up the hillside, with splendid views to the east towards Amalfi and beyond. • After about 200m/yds, the path turns left, passes old houses and continues as a field path for 400m/yds, to an isolated old pylon. Here go straight uphill to an iron gate in a wall and then half-left up to steps which lead to a narrow road by a ➤➤; turn right. After 400m/yds you reach a path junction with a cube-shaped concrete water supply building on the left.

38 Amalfi road tunnel (west end) — Tovere (east side)

This route provides the essential link between Amalfi and the Conca dei Marini hillside, with minimal road-walking. Affording extensive views, it passes through pleasant villages, under the brooding presence of the Santa Rosa Convent on its rocky perch to the west. You could eliminate some of the walking by taking the Agerola bus as far as the church in Vèttica Minore and pick up the route from there.

38a Amalfi road tunnel (west end) to Tovere (east side)

Time: 2h20min; *Grade:* moderate, with a *height gain* of 380m/1250ft

From the western end of the road tunnel, take the narrow road (Via Maestra dei Villaggi) that rises gently between apartments. It shortly narrows into a path which is followed for 1.5km/1mi (generally uphill) to Lone's cemetery. En route you pass the small chapel of La Carmine and a look-out under Lone's chapel; soon after this, the path bends right; at the cemetery the path turns left and descends very steeply to the Agerola road. • Turn right up the road, round the bend to the left and, at the next right-hand bend, take the path uphill to the left (Salita San Pietro a Gudaro). Very soon go right, climbing up more steps. These lead up and round to the left, to the church of San Michele at Vèttica Minore. Pass below the church, then walk up to the road. • Turn left on the road for 40m/yds, then go right up more steps (Via Maestra dei Villaggi; ignore the 'privato' sign). Take steps up to cross a minor road, and then follow broad zigzags up the mountainside. The path makes a broad sweep up to the left, to a path junction by a concrete water supply building.

38b Tovere (east side) to the Amalfi road tunnel (west end)

Time: 1h40min; *Grade:* easy, with a *descent* of 250m/820ft

From the path junction by a concrete water supply building, looking downhill, take the stepped path descending left across the open hillside. It later leads in broad zigzags down to a minor road and then down a few more steps to the Agerola road at Vèttica Minore. • Turn left along the road for 40m/yds, then right to pass below the church of San Michele. At first level, the path then descends to the right, to a T-junction. Here turn left to regain the road. Turn right down the road, go round the bend to the right and, just past the cemetery, take steep steps up to the left. • At the top of the steps turn right; after about 1.5km/1mi (generally descending), you reach the road tunnel.

Maiori/Minori

From each of these small towns a deep valley runs from the coast into the hinterland; the valleys are separated by a wooded ridge bearing the ruined convent of San Nicola. The Sambuco Valley behind Minori is only 4km/2.5mi long, ending at the mountain pass, Il Passo. The valley behind Maiori opens out after 6km/ 3.7mi to the wide undulating plain of Tramonti (photographs pages 32-33 and 136), itself divided by a ridge at the end which the cemetery of Santa Maria looks out over the region's 'capital', Polvica. Tramonti is bounded on the east by a rugged ridge of high mountains. On the most southerly of these, at a height of 870m/2900ft, is perched the Santuario dell'Avvocata, shown on page 97.

Getting about
The towns are served by the coastal service Amalfi/ Salerno. SITA also runs a service from Maiori to Tramonti, see details in Walk segments 43 and 44.

Tourist sights
Minori. Apart from the remains of a Roman villa with some fine mosaics, there is also a splendid large basilica on the east side of town, by the shady Piazza Cantilena.

Maiori. Some 4km/2.5mi along the coast road from Maiori towards Salerno a former abbey, Santa Maria de Olearia, houses some quite outstanding frescoes dating from the 12th century. See details in Walk segment 41.

WALK SEGMENTS
39 Minori — Maiori
A good path, separated from the busy coast road, connects these towns. It climbs quite high, but gives excellent views down to Minori and visits the 10th-century church of San Michele, with its little piazza looking out to sea. Photographs pages 90 and 98

39a Minori to Maiori
Time: 1h; *Grade:* moderate, with a *height gain* of 140m/460ft
From the basilica, set back from the eastern end of Minori's promenade, take the road under its tower, walking away from the coast. After 200m/yds, just past a modern school on the right, turn right up well-built

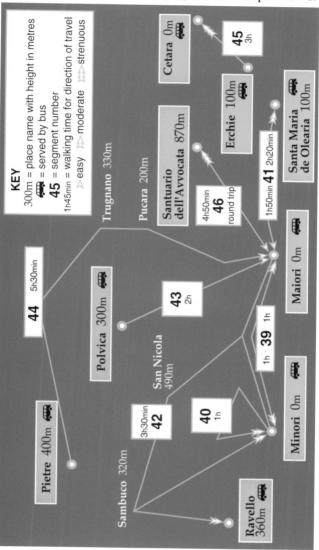

KEY
300m = place name with height in metres
🚌 = served by bus
45 = segment number
1h45min = walking time for direction of travel
▷ easy ▷▷ moderate ▷▷▷ strenuous

Cetara 0m 🚌

45 3h

Erchie 100m 🚌

Santa Maria de Olearia 100m 🚌

Trugnano 330m

Pucara 200m

Santuario dell'Avvocata 870m

4h50min **46** round trip

1h50min **41** 2h20min

Maiori 0m 🚌

Polvica 300m 🚌

43 2h

San Nicola 490m

1h - **39** 1h

44 5h30min

Pietre 400m 🚌

3h30min **42**

Sambuco 320m

40 1h

Minori 0m 🚌

Ravello 360m 🚌

steps. Beyond a few zigzags, at a junction (↔), turn right (signposted to Convento San Nicola, San Michele, Maiori). Some 100m/yds further on there is an excellent viewpoint (↔) over Minori. Continue up more steps to the church of San Michele (you are now in the hamlet of Torre). Continue past the church, bend to the left, then go up more steps, to a prominent junction by railings. [**Walk segment 42** goes up left here.] • Continue on a generally level path, through a wide right-hand bend; then descend into Maiori. On coming to a large church, go right round the back of it and descend to the main road, then turn right to the sea-front.

39b Maiori to Minori

Time: 1h; *Grade:* moderate, with a *height gain* of 140m/460ft

From the statue of Mother and Child on the sea-front in Maiori, follow the broad road inland for 200m/yds, to a small triangular piazza on the left (Raffaele d'Amato). Turn left, ascend to the right of the large church, and continue up the path (Via Vena), gently climbing the hillside. The path rises for 400m/yds, then bends right into a side-valley. After sweeping left to the far side of the valley, you come to a prominent junction by railings. [**Walk segment 42** goes up to the right here.] • The path to Minori continues ahead and soon bends right to the church of San Michele. Continue down to a fine viewpoint (➳) above Minori and to the town. On reaching a road, turn left to the basilica and Piazza Cantilena.

40 Minori Circuit

If you have an hour to spare and would like to get good view of Minori and its setting, then this circuit is ideal.

Time: 1h; *Grade:* moderate, with a *height gain* of 150m/500ft

From the basilica, set back from the eastern end of Minori's promenade, take the road under its tower,

walking away from the coast. After 200m/yds, just past a modern school on the right, turn right up well-built steps. Beyond a few zigzags, you come to a junction (➳). Continue uphill to the left (Via Torre Annunziata). The path soon

Overlooking the sea, this small piazza by the 10th-century church of San Michele, lies on the path between Maiori and Minori (Walk segment 39, Excursion 9).

steepens and climbs a long flight of steps. After passing an old tower, you come to a bend to the left. • Almost immediately, turn left on a gently-descending path. This sweeps to the left for 300m/yds, giving a bird's-eye view of Minori and the hillside up to Ravello. After going into and out of the side-valley and descending some steps, you come to a prominent junction. You can descend to the left here but, to extend the walk a little further, go right uphill for a short way, then follow the path down to a motor road in the town and turn left to the sea-front.

41 Maiori — Santa Maria de Olearia

*The frescoes in the 12th-century monastery of Santa Maria give a splendid focus to this walk. The monastery was founded by monks who came from the eastern Mediterranean, and the frescoes echo the style of those seen, for example, in Meteor, Greece. You can take the bus to the monastery or back, if you wish; the bus stop bears the name of the monastery and is the next stop after Maiori cemetery, some 4km along the road to Salerno from Maiori. Telephone AST Maiori on 089877452 to ask for opening times. The AST lies next door but one to the Bar Oriente. The walk itself takes a route parallel with the coast road and high above it, mostly on a mule track; it traverses a wild hillside of myrtle and white heather, with extensive views along the coast. **Photographs pages 14 and 92***

41a Maiori to Santa Maria de Olearia

Time: 2h20min; *Grade:* moderate, with a *height gain* of 260m/850ft
From the Bar Oriente near the eastern end of the sea-front in Maiori, follow the road inland for 200m/yds. Where the road bends left, fork right into Via de Iosola. After 100m/yds, at a T-junction, turn right; 30m/yds further on, by a ••, turn left up Via Grade dei Pezzi. By always ascending and taking the obvious path ahead, you emerge from the houses, swing to the right and climb (with a wall on the right), after 800m/0.5mi coming to a prominently-sited isolated pink and white house (No 5). • Pass the house [**Walk segment 46** leaves up steps to the left]. Continue on the now-level path, which will contour into and out of the next wide side-valley, rising and falling slightly. You will emerge at a fork of tracks 1.2km/0.7mi further on — it can already been seen ahead, on the same contour. On reaching the fork, go left uphill on a wide mule track. Already high above the coast road, this track climbs another 400m/yds, up to a junction by low woven-wattle walls retaining the hillside. Continue round to the right, soon beginning a gradual descent. After a further 1km/0.6mi along the wide mule track, you reach a house with a high mesh fence by some

Fresco at Santa Maria de Olearia (Walk segment 41)

abandoned cars. You have passed above Maiori's cemetery. • Just beside the house, take the track that descends quite steeply; initially it runs straight down the hillside, then bends to the right. After 150m/yds, you come to a lower wide mule track. Follow it to the right, down some zigzags, to the coast road. Turn left along the road and walk into a side-valley. The monastery of Santa Maria de Olearia is on the left, 300m/yds beyond the second bend in the side-valley.

41b Santa Maria de Olearia to Maiori
Time: 1h50min; *Grade:* easy, with a *height gain* of 120m/395ft and a descent of 200m/660ft

Turn right out of the monastery of Santa Maria, to descend the coast road for 300m/yds through a side valley. Go round two left-hand bends: 100m/yds beyond the second bend, climb a short flight of steps up to the right. The path leads past a lime kiln to a steep mule track which takes you in zigzags up the hillside for 200m/yds. The track then swings right and climbs more gently. Then, where the main track bends right, climb the steep rocky track straight ahead. This bends right and leads after 150m/yds to a higher wide mule track, by a house and some abandoned cars. • Turn left here. The track now contours the hillside ascending gently for 1km/0.6mi, to a fork by low woven-wattle walls retaining the hillside. Go left now, gently downhill. In a further 400m/yds the path descends to a narrow gravel road, at the start of a wide side-valley. Continue to the right. This road (later reverting to path) will contour into and out of the side-valley for 1.2km/0.7mi, emerging at the isolated pink and white house which can be seen ahead. [**Walk segment 46** joins here.] • On reaching the house, descend the steps beyond it, bending to the right. Descend for 800m/0.5mi, always keeping ahead at the few junctions encountered. The path curves to the left and arrives in Maiori: descend steps between houses for 100m/yds, turn right at a junction by a ↦ and, after a further 30m/yds, go left on Via de Iosola. This leads to a road to the sea-front.

42 Minori or Maiori to Ravello or Minori, via San Nicola and Sambuco

The now-abandoned convent of San Nicola sits on a high hilltop above Minori and Maiori, looking out over the Bay of Salerno and ringed by higher mountains. A good path makes its way quite easily from Minori or Maiori up to the building, although the climb is relatively prolonged Having enjoyed the view from the convent, you can either retrace your steps or go on to the pleasant little farming village of Sambuco and take a valley walk back to Minori. From Sambuco you also have the option of taking the minor road to Ravello.

Time: 3h30min; *Grade:* moderate, with a *height gain* of 490m/1600ft

Take **Walk segment 39a** (from Minori) or **39b** (from Maiori) to the path starting at the railings. Turn uphill. • You now stay on this path for about 2km/1.2mi, often climbing steps, keeping near the top of the ridge or on its left side, moving from housing into pine and then other woods. Excellent views accompany you. Eventually, having passed below and to the left of San Nicola, you come to the top of the climb. Here turn sharp right for 300m/yds, to reach the convent and admire the view, then return to the main path. Turn sharp left to return the way you came. • Or, to continue via Sambuco, turn half-right, on a broad, gently descending track along the ridge. After 300m/yds, at a ruined building, turn half-left down a prominent mule track; it takes you down to the stream below Sambuco and up concrete steps to the road. • Turn left for 400m/yds along the road to a SITA bus stop and turning place. From here you could continue along the road to Ravello (on reaching the main road, cross directly to pick up the narrow road then path via Lacco, **Walk segment 8b**). To descend to Minori, after 50m/yds further on the road fork left down a path. This leads to steps that are the start of the path down the valley back to Minori. Just keep straight ahead all the way. When you meet the first road in Minori, turn left, then go right round a bend and follow the road straight ahead through the town, to the coast road.

43 Polvica to Maiori

Walk segments 43 and 44 explore the high farming area of Tramonti. Ringed by high mountains, the area feels quite different from the coast. For one thing the risk of winter frost forbids growth of the ubiquitous lemon trees of the coast; here you see only vines on the pergolas. The viticulture demonstrates self-sufficiency: by each vineyard you will see willow stumps, the new fronds being clipped each autumn to bind the vines to the pergolas. The pergolas themselves come from the mountainsides, where you will see large areas of coppiced chestnut and alder, grown just to provide this sort of timber, and enormous stockpiles of harvested poles (see photograph on pages 32-33). Not only fruit, you see all sorts of vegetables in the small fields — aubergines, peppers, and many kinds of beans. In autumn tomatoes will be hung to dry. Everywhere the small three-wheeler 'scooter' lorry is to be seen, which has largely, but not completely, supplanted the mule. • This walk takes you in easy stages from the 'capital' of Tramonti down to the coast at Maiori and gives you a good feel for the area. Perhaps half the distance is covered on almost traffic-free minor roads. Walk segment 44 provides a lengthier excursion and an even better insight. • To get to Polvica, take the 09.00 Tramonti bus from Amalfi via Maiori. At other times, take the Tramonti bus from outside the AST near the eastern end of the promenade in Maiori (SITA tickets from the Bar Oriente next door but one). The AST has up-to-date timetables. After the bus turns left off the main road to descend and climb out of a small gorge, alight immediately on reaching houses; this is Polvica. Photographs below and page 136

Time: 2h; *Grade:* easy

Taking the bus driver's view as you enter Polvica, take the first road immediately on the left (just after the

Municipio building). This bends right after 100m/yds and descends to a bridge. Just after the bridge, take the first path up left; at a fence, go half-right. On regaining the road, turn left. • Now keeping on the right-hand side of the valley, follow the wider road for 1km/0.6mi. At a fork just before a church, go left down a narrow road; pass below the church and, after 100m/yds, fork left down the minor road. After 300m/yds, just after the first building on the left, turn right. Then go straight ahead, to join a path which starts by crossing a small bridge. This runs mostly level for 300m/yds and then goes into and out of a side

Walk segment 43: lemon trees overhang a typical narrow road in the lower part of the Tramonti region.

valley. As you come up to the church of Paterno Sant'Elia, there is a splendid picnic spot in a small piazza, complete with seats in sun or shade, ↤↦ and magnificent view. • Climb to the church and join an asphalt road; follow this for 500m/yds, to where it bends sharp left. Here take the path up to the right of the house and round a side-valley. [Just before you reach the ridge bounding the south side of this valley, **Walk segment 44** joins from the left.] • Round the ridge to the right and take a path below a house. After 250m/yds, you come to the end of a terrace (on your right). Here descend steps half-left and walk alongside a lower terrace. At its end, by a stout structure of poles, turn right and contour (gently descending) into and out of a further side-valley, coming to the upper houses of Ponteprimario. Descend between the houses, always going left at junctions. At the bottom, turn left into the little piazza with its memorial to the citizens of the village lost to flooding in the mid-1950s (on a night after it had rained incessantly for 48 hours). Then turn right and descend the valley to Maiori, using the minor road which lies to the west of the main road. At one point this road is interrupted by a garden centre with large grille gates; the path goes right on top of a low wall to rejoin the road. As you descend, look up at the southernmost mountain on the eastern side, to spot the sanctuary of Avvocata (Walk segment 46) just below the summit.

44 Pietre to Maiori

This all-day walk provides a very pleasant and easy, if lengthy, ramble through the backwaters of Tramonti, mostly on paths and tracks, and always with the magnificent mountain backdrop. See Walk segment 43 (page 93) for general comments on Tramonti and its bus service. Buses from Maiori continue beyond Polvica to the next village, Pietre. If the bus continues to Capitignano (check timetable or ask driver) alight here. Sometimes the bus first makes a short detour right from Polvica up to Corsano and back, before continuing to Pietre. Photograph pages 32-33

Time: 5h30min; *Grade:* easy, with a *height gain* of 300m/980ft in short stages

From the centre of Pietre, take the road to the right (north) through the village for 500m/yds to a join a wide road. Go left. After 300m/yds more pass the church of Capitignano on the right, and 100m/yds further on, turn sharp left up a narrow road by a ↤↦. The Capitignano stop is 100m/yds beyond this turning. After 200m/yds this changes into a mule track,

sweeps to the right and climbs continuously for another 700m/yds up to a main road. Here turn right immediately onto a level asphalted road. Follow this for 2.6km/1.6mi along the crest that splits the Tramonti Plain. You reach Santa Maria di Tramonti — a cemetery sited just at the end of the ridge.
• From the cemetery, retrace your route for 10 minutes to the fork in the road; here take a mule track down to the right. On reaching a minor road turn left. After 100m/yds go right over a bridge and, after 400m/yds (50m/yds after the first house on the right), turn right down a steep asphalted road; after a further 50m/yds, turn left between houses. Shortly you find yourself on a pleasant path with an excellent embankment overlooking a stream. The path continues down to the stream and curves up right to the houses of Trugnano. • Continue straight ahead within Trugnano; a road joins from left and after 300m/yds departs again to the left. Continue straight ahead down a narrow lane. After another 200m/yds you can see the ornate campanile and church in Campinola. The lane ends at gates. Go through the gates and up an asphalt drive for 100m/yds, then turn sharp right onto a level path which becomes paved under vines. Continue ahead up to the main road. Turn right and walk through and out of Casa Vaccaro for 800m/0.5mi, to a sharp right-hand bend by a hardware shop. Turn left up a narrow road between houses. This levels out and is the start of a traverse of the left-hand side of the valley — through the villages of Gete, Pendolo and Novella. By Gete church there is chapel in a grotto (signposted), worth a look. Always go ahead at junctions, the way fluctuating between road, track and path — sometimes a bit overgrown. • On arriving at Pucara church with its onion-dome down a steep alley, go left along a level alley to pick up a narrow road leading down to the main road. Immediately cross onto a minor road going right, signed 'Paterno'. After 300m/yds on this road, turn left in front of a mill (Carto-technica Civale), cross a footbridge, and take steps down left to the riverside path. After 300m/yds, at a gravel road junction, take the stepped mule track ahead up into the woods. Ascend this for 400m/yds, slope up to the left until, after a few zigzags, you join a higher path. Turn left and continue on **Walk segment 43**.

45 Erchie to Cetara

This most easterly of the walks in this guide traverses a little-walked ridge down to the pleasant fishing village of Cetara. The walk starts on the coast road above Erchie, at the next stop after the easily recognised Capo d'Orso stop — the highest point on the road out of Maiori, with a resturant of the same name. Our stop comes some 1.8km further on, just after the road has turned inland after going parallel with the coast. The route ascends a valley on a very stony mule track, takes a good path up the ridge and has an easy mule track for the descent. Excellent views to Salerno with its backdrop of mountains.

Time: 3h *Grade:* Strenuous, with *height gain* of 340m/1100ft and *descent* of 430m/1400ft

From the layby with the bus stop, take the intially surfaced road up left and then right to some never-to-be-finished buildings. Pass to the left and then between them, to pick up a well-used mule track that follows a wall on your right. This stony track ascends the left-hand side of a large valley, with the slope up to your left. After **45min**, round a spur below a ruined building. Fifteen minutes later more ruins are reached, with a fork in the track behind them (**1h**). • Fork right onto a level path, cross a stream, and ascend the bare rocky hillside above by a path that zigzags between and across the outcrops of rock. Near the top of the rocky area be alert to the path striking off to the right. This well-trampled path now continues between grasses and shrubs for some 200m/yds, taking a wide curve to the left. • On meeting a broad mule track, turn right. This track takes you to Cetara. First it traverses the head of shallow valley, to a ruin. Then it descends the side of the next valley, initially to the left and then to the

The sanctuary of Avvocata lies on a shelf almost 900m/3000ft above the coast (Walk segment 46).

right, down to Cetara. Much of the descent takes the form of wooden-edged gravel steps. In Cetara the bus stop is where you meet the main road; there's a bar overlooking the beach and harbour.

46 Maiori — Santuario dell'Avvocata — Maiori

If you have spent any time near the coast east of Amalfi, you will have seen the large Avvocata monastery perched on its eyrie, a shelf just below the summit of the most easterly of the coastal mountains. It looks down on

Minori, seen from the path to Maiori (Walk segment 39)

Maiori from a height of 873m/2860ft, beckoning any keen hill-walker. It opens at Pentecost for a service, and a few other times each year. The path up is well-used but very rough in places, a route for experienced well-shod walkers. **Photographs page 14 and 97**

Time: 4h50min; *Grade:* strenuous, with a *height gain* and *descent* of 870m/2850ft

Take **Walk segment 41a** (page 91) up to the pink and white house (**20min**). Pass to the right of the house and immediately take the concrete steps ascending to the left. At the top of them, you begin a long ascent up the left-hand side of the valley ahead on a rocky path. For much of the time an old water duct and two black plastic pipes accompany you on your left. Finally the path reaches the valley floor and then ascends the other side, to a small grassy promontory where there is an all-but-abandoned building with a double, rounded roof (**1h25min**). • Climb the heavily-used path directly beyond the building, to reach an old lime kiln (**1h 40min**), then a seat, a shrine and a spring (**1h55min**), and finally a picnic table on the right in the woods (**2h05min**). From here the path turns left and a liberal sprinkling of yellow spots (over-painted in red) guides you up to the Santuario dell'Avvocata (**2h40min**).

For the descent, as a reminder: follow yellow dots (over-painted in red) down to a picnic site with a table in the woods on the left (**30min**). Continue down to the right on the main, heavily-used path — to a seat, a shrine and a spring (**40min**). Continue straight on down to an old lime kiln (**50min**), go round its lower end, and continue descending to a small grassy promontory, where there is a forlorn building with a double, rounded roof (**1h**). • Go down the narrow path on the right-hand side of the building, to the nearby valley floor, and cross the stream. You will now descend the right-hand side of this valley down to an isolated pink and white house (**1h50min**). From here take **Walk segment 41b** (page 92) down to Maiori (**2h10min**).

❋ Sorrento

The bustling town of Sorrento lies on a broad shelf 70m/230ft above the sea. To the south and west the terrain (both cultivated and wooded) rises quite steeply, eventually to a height of 400m/1300ft. Here, on the crest of the peninsula, lies the village of Sant'Agata. The ridge continues southwest to the tip of the peninsula, rising to a maximum height of 500m/1650ft at Monte San Costanzo, near the village of Termini. The elegant small town of Massa Lubrense sits a little above the coast, on the west of the peninsula.

As the slopes are less steep than on the Amalfi Coast, the paths here consist less often of steps. Despite more development and road-building than on the Amalfi Coast, the path network is surprisingly complete and offers excellent walking with frequent panoramic views. Beware wet weather as, even on the easy paths, you will need shoes with a good tread to prevent slipping on steep stone paving.

You may wish to obtain the excellent walking map covering the area which is referred to on page 19. The routes described here use parts of the paths on this map, but do not follow the colour-coded paths exactly. Be guided by this book, *not* the coloured waymarks or the ceramic tiles at path junctions.

Getting about

Buses. To get the best out of the walking behind Sorrento, you will need to master the SITA bus services which radiate from the Circumvesuviana railway station (Timetables 8-10, pages 131-132). Tickets are available from the newspaper shop at the station or, if it is closed, from the bar, just to the left on the station approach road. Obtain a photocopy of the current bus timetables from the official tourist office (AST). These repay careful study, as they provide a complex pattern of service to the towns and villages where the walk segments start. For Walk segments 63, 64 and 65, you may wish instead to ride to the Colli di San Pietro stop (Timetable 2), or take the Circumvesuviana bus service from Piano direct to Colli di Fontanelle (Timetable 11). See Timetable 13 for notes on Sorrento town buses.

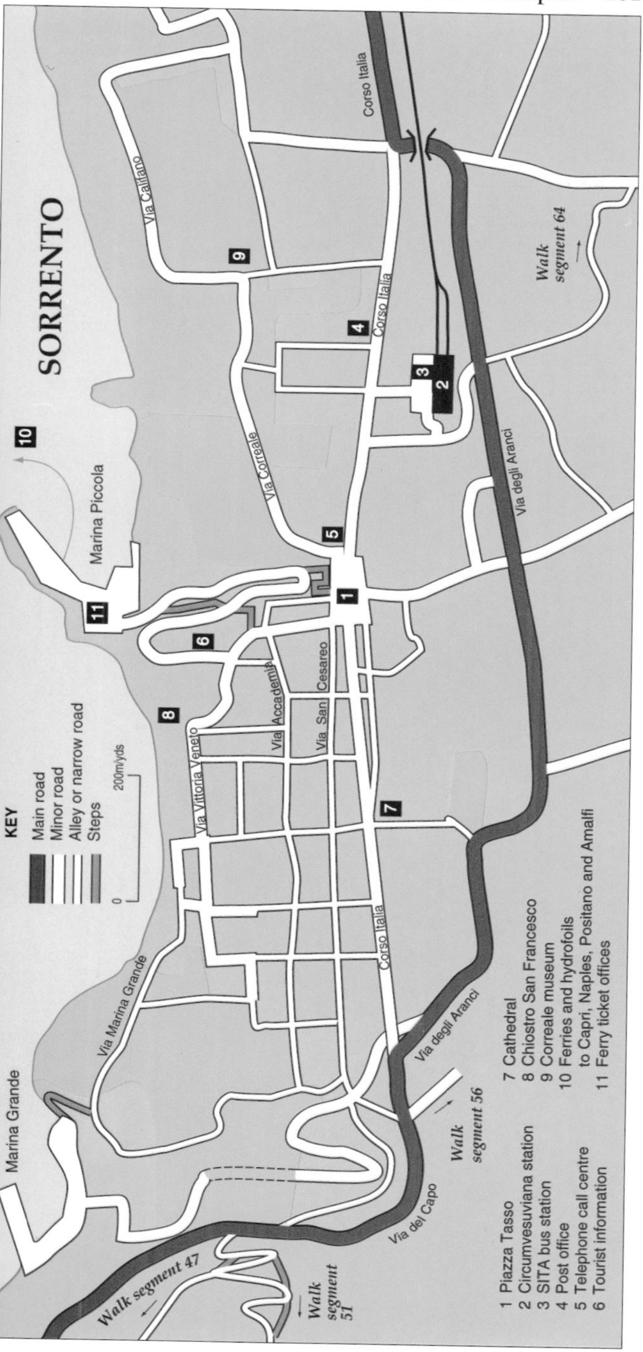

SORRENTO

Marina Grande

Marina Piccola

KEY
Main road
Minor road
Alley or narrow road
Steps

0   200m/yds

Via Caliano

Corso Italia

Via Correale

Via degli Aranci

Via Marina Grande

Via Vittoria Veneto

Via Accademia

Via San Cesareo

Corso Italia

Via degli Aranci

Via del Capo

Walk segment 64

Walk segment 56

Walk segment 51

Walk segment 47

1 Piazza Tasso
2 Circumvesuviana station
3 SITA bus station
4 Post office
5 Telephone call centre
6 Tourist information
7 Cathedral
8 Chiostro San Francesco
9 Correale museum
10 Ferries and hydrofoils
    to Capri, Naples, Positano and Amalfi
11 Ferry ticket offices

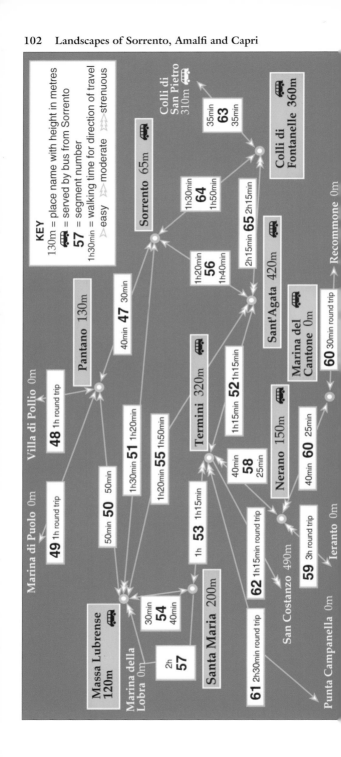

Tourist sights

The old town, west of the Piazza Tasso, is delightful to stroll around. Visit, too, the medieval cathedral, the Palazzo Correale and its museum (set in pleasant gardens with a fine view of the Bay of Naples), and the church of San Francesco, with its beautiful cloisters and gardens. All of these buildings are centrally located.

Walk planning tips

The paths immediately to the west of Sorrento offer some pleasant walks going directly from town; choose from the Walk planner. For easy walks see excursions 13 to 15 on page 23.

To walk further afield, it is best to take the bus. Choose Termini or Nerano for coastal walks (Walk segments 58 to 62). From Termini a splendid chain of paths leads back to Sorrento via Massa Lubrense and Sant'Agata (Walk segments 53, 54, 55 and 56), and these segments can be joined by bus at the intermediate points, if a shorter walk is preferred. The coastal walk from Colli di Fontanelle (Walk segment 65) is fine, as is the walk back to Sorrento from there (Walk segment 64). If you are staying in Sorrento, consider walking in the Positano area and on Capri.

WALK SEGMENTS

47 Sorrento — Pantano

This segment takes you west out of Sorrento, avoiding main roads. It links to Walk segment 50 for Massa Lubrense and opens up other possibilities — perhaps a visit to the Villa Pollio, a Roman villa on a headland, with wide views of the Bay of Naples, or to Marina di Puolo, a pleasant small fishing village. **Photographs pages 12 and 104**

47a Sorrento to Pantano

Time: 40min; *Grade:* easy, with a *height gain* of 70m/230ft

From Piazza Tasso in Sorrento, take Via San Cesareo (if Signor Tasso's marble lips could move he would say: 'from here, take the second left'). After 600m/0.35mi, at its end, turn right and then immediately left. This road leads up to the main road west out of Sorrento. • Turn right on the road and, after 50m/yds, turn left up a cobbled road opposite 'International Camping'. Go round the hairpin bend and take the path on the right, to short-cut the next hairpin. In a further 100m/yds, at a three-way fork (superb view from here of Sorrento and the Bay of Naples), take the left fork (to the left of Hotel Badia) — a footpath between walls which leads

Descending from Pantano to Sorrento; Vesuvius is the landmark across the Bay of Naples (Walk segment 47).

up to a higher main road after 200m/yds. • Go right along main road for 100m/yds then take a narrow road on the left (Via Pantano, with metal railings at the outset). Follow it round bends and through olive groves, contouring for 1km/0.6mi, until a narrow road descends on the right and cast-iron street lamps start. Continue level round a right-hand bend, to a junction with a wider road on a bend; this is Pantano.

47b Pantano to Sorrento
Time: 30min; *Grade:* easy

Facing the olive grove at Pantano, take the narrow road right. Keep level round bends and through olive groves. After 1km/0.6mi, on reaching a main road, go right. After 100m/yds, turn half-left down a path. Now forking downhill at each junction, you reach a lower main road. • Turn right and after only 50m/yds turn left down steps. These merge with a minor road which takes you to a crossroads on the edge of Sorrento town centre. Go right, then immediately left; after 50m/yds you have two options to get to the town centre: go straight ahead or else turn left, for a more scenic route with views over the coast.

48 Pantano — Villa di Pollio
An 'out and back' visit to the Roman villa on the coast.

Time: 1h round trip; *Grade:* easy, with a *height gain* of 100m/330ft

Facing the olive grove, descend the road left, to the main road. Cross this and walk down the minor road going seaward (Transversa Punta Capo). This splendid cobbled road heads straight downhill to the headland (Punta del Capo) and its villa (Villa di Pollio). There is also a little inlet of the sea here which glimmers in the most beautiful of translucent colours. Return by the same route.

49 Pantano — Marina di Puolo
An 'out and back' visit to Marina di Puolo, a pleasant little fishing village with bars and a restaurant.

Time: 1h round trip; *Grade:* easy, with a *height gain* of 100m/330ft

Facing the olive grove, descend the road left, to the main road. Turn left here and, after 200m/yds, turn right by the Hotel Dania; there is a rusty sign for Marina di Puolo here. Go left behind the hotel; this alley meets a minor road after 400m/yds; turn right and follow the road down to the fishing village of Marina di Puolo. Return by the same route.

50 Pantano—Massa Lubrense

Combined with Walk segment 47, this segment gives a low-level connection between Sorrento and Massa Lubrense.

50a Pantano to Massa Lubrense

Time: 50min; *Grade:* easy, with a *height gain* of 50m/170ft

Ascend the wide road by Stations of the Cross on the left. At station number four, fork right down a narrow road which, after 100m/yds, becomes a footpath. Curve round to the right and ascend to a narrow road. Continue ahead on this for 800m/ 0.5mi, mainly level, to a T-junction at a hairpin bend. Descend right for 50m/yds to the next bend, and take the earthen path on the left. This descends in 150m/yds to the main road, the last stretch down a flight of steps. • Turn left on the main road. Go round a bend to the right and one to the left. Fork left up a paved path (Via San Montano). Zigzag up to pass by a large house and join a narrow road. Follow this for 500m/yds, going straight on at a junction, until it joins a main road entering Massa Lubrense.

50b Massa Lubrense to Pantano

Time: 50min; *Grade:* easy, with a *height gain* of 50m/170ft

From the cathedral and *Municipio* building, ascend the wide street to the triangle of roads. Turn left along the main road and, after 100m/yds, fork left onto a narrow road (Via Molini). Follow this for 500m/yds, going half-left at a junction (still on Via Molini), until it ends at a large house. Continue on a path beside the house, down to the main road. • Turn right and go round a bend to the right and most of one to the left. Here ascend a flight of narrow steps, then take a path rising to the left. Meeting a road, go right and, after 50m/yds, go ahead on a narrow road (Via Vigliano). Follow this, mainly level, for 800m/0.5mi, until a few steps take you down to a path which curves left round a valley. Now join the start of a narrow road and, after

100m/yds, turn left down a wide road. After 100m/yds this bends left in front of an olive grove and a narrow road goes right. This is Pantano.

51 Sorrento — Massa Lubrense

Massa Lubrense and Sorrento lie only 4km apart so, instead of going by bus, why not take this walk amid olive groves and gardens?

51a Sorrento to Massa Lubrense

Time: 1h30min; *Grade:* moderate, with a *height gain* of 160m/530ft

From Sorrento, follow **Walk segment 47a** (page 103) up the cobbled road opposite 'International Camping'. Keep ahead round all hairpin bends (three short-cut paths), until the road climbs straight away from Sorrento. After 150m/yds the road turns left; here go straight ahead on a path (Via Priora) to the main road. Cross it and climb Via Priora, at first steeply and then more gently, continuing straight ahead for 1km/0.6mi. From the top of the hill, continue ahead for 400m/yds, to a crossroads by a Madonna and Cherubs shrine. Go straight over to join Via Bagnulo. After 350m/yds, after walking under an arch beneath a white house, take the first right. This road descends round two bends, after 150m/yds reaching a T-junction: turn left. After 150m/yds take the first right, then continue straight ahead to the centre of Massa Lubrense.

51b Massa Lubrense to Sorrento

Time: 1h20min; *Grade:* easy, with a *height gain* of 110m/360ft

From Massa Lubrense, follow **Walk segment 54b** (page 109) to Via Rachione. Keep up this road for 250m/yds. On meeting a road, cross it and climb Via Bagnulo. At a T-junction turn left. After 150m/yds (where the way ahead is an earthen path), follow the road up to the right, rounding two bends. At a T-junction turn left. • After 350m/yds, at a crossroads, go ahead on Via Monte Corbo. After another 400m/yds of gentle climbing, you reach the top of the hill by a Madonna and Cherubs shrine. Continue ahead for 1km/0.6mi, descending to the main road at a hairpin bend. Cross straight over onto a path and continue downhill, to join Via Capodimonte. Shortly this road descends in a series of hairpin bends to the main road (short-cut paths, and superb views of Sorrento and the Bay of Naples). • Turn right and after only 50m/yds turn left down steps. These widen out into a minor road. At a crossroads on the edge of Sorrento, go right, then immediately left; after 50m/yds, you have two options to reach the town centre: go straight ahead, or turn left for a more scenic route, with views over the coast.

52 Sant'Agata — Termini

This walk segment takes a snaking line which crosses the main road between the two towns four times. Our route goes over three hilltops, with superb wide views over the peninsula and the bays on either side. **Photograph pages 26-27**

52a Sant'Agata to Termini

Time: 1h15min; *Grade:* easy, with a *height gain* of 80m/260ft

Facing the Hotel delle Palme, turn left and after 100m/yds turn right into Via Reola. Immediately turn left (direction Termini, Via dei Campi) and follow the road in a right bend past the supermarket. After 150m/yds more, where the main road bends left, take the narrow road ascending the hill straight ahead (by the start of Via Castagneto). After 500m/yds the minor road rejoins the main road by the chapel of Santa Maria della Neve. Walk on the main road past the cemetery on the left and then immediately take *not* Via Torvillo, but the next road which forks left and descends. On reaching the main road again after 200m/yds, cross into Via Monte Arso. After 40m/yds do not take Via Monte Orso, but stay on Via Monte Arso. Walk down to the main road again and turn right on this, until after 150m/yds (just past a restaurant), turn left onto Via Colarusso. After 100m/yds bend right at a junction and continue over the hill, to reach the main road again. Go straight over (Via delle Tore) and after 600m/ 0.35mi fork left on a narrow road which leads over the hill ahead. The road reduces in stages to a path which leads to the road again. Turn left into Termini.

52b Termini to Sant'Agata

Time: 1h15min; *Grade:* easy, with a *height gain* of 100m/330ft

Follow **Walk segment 53a** to reach the crest of a hill and go down to a wide road. Turn right and after 600m/0.35mi cross over the main road into Via Tuoro. Go over the hill ahead and descend to a T-junction; here turn left to rejoin the main road. Turn right and, after 150m/yds (just after a crossroads), fork left to ascend Via Monte Arso. On reaching the main road again, cross onto a path (still Via Monte Arso, may be over-grown) which leads up to the main road again. Turn right and, immediately after the chapel of Santa Maria della Neve, fork left onto a minor road. This leads in 500m/yds over a low hill to the main road again. Walk straight ahead to the centre of Sant'Agata.

53 Termini — Santa Maria

The small village of Termini sits high up near the tip of the Sorrento Peninsula. It commands splendid views of Capri, while itself being dominated by a hill on which is perched the church of San Costanzo. The village, served by bus, is a good starting point for walks down to the coast, and for a chain of segments to take you back to Sorrento, of which this is the first. • *This segment follows ancient mule tracks through the sleepy villages of Schiazzano and Santa Maria. The tracks are now often concreted, but in many places are still paved, stepped, or even earthen. Always the views are rewarding; local agriculture and gardening can be observed first hand.* **Photograph pages 26-27**

53a Termini to Santa Maria
Time: 1h; *Grade:* easy, with a *height gain* of 20m/65ft

Leave the main square of Termini by ascending the stone-paved Via delle Torre to the left of the restaurant. Go round a bend to the left and soon take steps up to the right (on the far side of a building, the Casearina Sorrentina). • After only 100m/yds, the path leads to the crest of a hill, from where there is a fine view of Capri and the Bay of Naples — the picnic spot shown on pages 26-27. Soon an earthen track comes underfoot, then concrete. Some 800m/0.5mi after leaving Termini, you reach a wide road: turn right. • After only 100m/yds, just past a house on the left, turn left down a steep narrow track with paving in its centre. Soon this track bends right; follow it to the centre of Schiazzano. In the village, turn left to the main square (bar, pizzeria, shop). • Leave the square on Via Santa Maria; soon it bends right and leaves the village. Notice now the coppiced sweet chestnut woodland on the right — producing poles for use in the vineyards and lemon groves. The pleasant path descends, then climbs again, up to the centre of Santa Maria. Make your way to the front of its large cream-coloured church.

53b Santa Maria to Termini
Time: 1h15min; *Grade:* moderate, with a *height gain* of 140m/460ft

From Santa Maria take the road at the left-hand side of the cream-coloured church. At the back of the church, go right on a narrow road, descending gradually to a stream, beyond which a path leads you up to the main square of Schiazzano (bar, pizzeria, shop). Take the narrow stone-paved road half-right out of the square; after 100m/yds turn right up another narrow road (Via Tore di Casa). • After 500m/yds, you reach a wide road: turn right and, 100m/yds further on, go left up an asphalt track. This reduces to a path as it crosses a low hill (photograph pages 26-27). On reaching a road, turn left to Termini.

54 Santa Maria — Massa Lubrense

This is the second segment in the chain from Termini to Sorrento. From Santa Maria you can make a pleasant detour to Annunziata by following Walk segment 57 for a short way and then retracing your steps.

54a Santa Maria to Massa Lubrense
Time: 30min; *Grade:* easy

From Santa Maria, with the front door of the church on your right, take the old paved road ahead. This soon bends left around the last building in the village and then gently descends on steps. After 300m/yds take the Via Sant'Agniello Vecchio, a narrow path forking off right between a high concrete wall on the right and the low boundary fence of a house. Some 200m/yds further on, you pass an excellent picnic spot in an olive grove, with good views over Massa Lubrense and the Bay of Naples. • After a further 100m/yds, at a junction of paths, note the small private chapel of the de Martino family on the left. Go straight on at the junction. After a further 250m/yds, you come to another junction (the other end of the Via Sant' Agniello Vecchio; there is a sign on the wall). [If you wish to skip Massa Lubrense and continue direct to Sant'Agata on **Walk segment 55a**, turn right here.] • To get to the centre of Massa Lubrense, turn left 30m/yds further on. Then continue for another 200m/yds, gently descending to a T-junction. A right turn, followed by left, leads to the town centre (all facilities here). The cathedral, *Municipio* and viewpoint are all further downhill.

54b Massa Lubrense to Santa Maria
Time: 40min; *Grade:* easy, with a *height gain* of 80m/260ft

Starting from the cathedral and *Municipio* in Massa Lubrense, take the wide street uphill, to the triangle in front of an imposing building. Walk along the right-hand side of the triangle and continue straight ahead up a narrow road (Via Rachione). Take first right, then the first left (Via Mortella). • After 200m/yds, at a T-junction, turn right. After 30m/yds this becomes Via Sant'Agniello Vecchio (there is a sign on the wall). [The path from Sant'Agata, **Walk segment 55**, comes in from the left here.] Continue along Via Sant'Agniello Vecchio for 250m/yds, to a junction of paths by a chapel (see notes in 54a above). Continue on a narrow path beside the chapel for another 300m/yds, through terraces, to a junction with a narrow road. Turn left up to Santa Maria.

55 Massa Lubrense — Sant'Agata

This is the third link in the chain of segments between Termini and Sorrento. (Or you could take Walk segment 51b for a direct connection to Sorrento, missing out Sant'Agata.) • This segment passes the gates of the Deserto Convent. A climb to the belvedere at the top of this building is worthwhile for the far-reaching views to Capri, the peninsula and the Bay of Naples. It is open 08.30-12.30 and 14.30-16.30 (Oct-March) or 16.00-20.00 (April-Sept). Ring the bell at the main door, enter on hearing the buzzer, and a nun will lend you the key. The belvedere is entered by the adjacent door. Free, but donation requested. You pass Sant'Agata's fine old church, too, famous for its inlaid marble altars.

55a Massa Lubrense to Sant'Agata

Time: 1h50min; *Grade:* moderate, with a *height gain* of 300m/980ft

From the cathedral and *Municipio* building in Massa Lubrense, follow **Walk segment 54b** (above) to Via Sant'Agniello Vecchio (there is a sign on the wall). Here Walk segment 54b continues ahead along Via Sant'Agniello Vecchio, but we turn left up another alley, after 100m/yds coming to a road. Cross straight over, then take Via San Francesco, an old paved path. Follow this uphill for 300m/yds, to the next road. Turn left for 50m/yds along this road and then go right up a continuation of Via San Francesco. (You could take a detour here, by going left along the road, to look at the church of San Francesco.) • After climbing the Via San Francesco (now a concrete track) for 150m/yds, turn right up Traversa San Francesco. This pleasant little path is a short-cut: it will bring you back onto the track higher up. Then continue for another 200m/yds, up to the next road (Via San Vito). Turn left and walk 400m/yds along the road to the church of San Vito (past an *alimentari* on the right). • Take the path (Via Tore al Deserto) at the right-hand side of the church. This paved path climbs for 350m/yds, then turns left along a drive for another 250m/yds, until a road is met at a T-junction. Turn right and follow this for 600m/yds, to a wide road at the gates of the Deserto Convent. Continue down the road past Sant'Agata's large old church and on to the centre of town.

55b Sant'Agata to Massa Lubrense

Time: 1h20min; *Grade:* easy

With your back to the Hotel delle Palme in the centre of Sant'Agata, take the road to the left, pass the large old church and walk uphill on Via Deserto. At a fork take the road to the right. On reaching the gates of the Deserto Convent after 800m/0.5mi, take the unnamed minor road down to the right. For 400m/yds, this undulates and then descends sharply. Some 100m/yds

The house where, in 1808, the King of Naples directed the siege of the English who were then occupying Capri (Walk segment 57)

after the start of the steep descent, turn left in front of a small walled-in olive grove. • This drive (Via Torre al Deserto), level at first, descends for 250m/yds to a fork in front of imposing house gates. Take the right-hand fork, going downhill at junctions on a paved path to the church of San Vito. Walk left along the road, away from the front of the church, for 400m/yds (passing an *alimentari* on your left). When the road bends sharply left, take a concrete track to the right, descending steeply. • Descend for 200m/yds, to where the track bends sharp right around the corner of a house. Here follow the well-used path straight ahead — a short-cut which curves right, to rejoin the track lower down. Continue down to a road. (A detour to the right here would take you to the church of San Francesco.) Turn left along road for 50m/yds and then turn right down a path. Follow the path downhill for 300m/yds, to the next road. • Go straight across the road and descend an alley, now with houses on your left, for 100m/yds. You come to a T-junction with the Via Sant' Agniello Vecchio (there is a sign on the wall on your left). [**Walk segment 54b** goes left here.] Go right for 30m/yds and then turn left. Continue for 200m/yds, gently descending to a T-junction. A right turn, followed by left, leads to the centre of Massa Lubrense (all town facilities). The cathedral, *Municipio* and viewpoint are further downhill.

56 Sant'Agata — Sorrento

This lovely gentle downhill walk takes old mule paths and alleys and culminates with the descent of the zigzag path from the chapel of Santa Maria Dolorata and its fourteen Stations of the Cross. You will have splendid views over Sorrento and the Bay of Naples.

56a Sant'Agata to Sorrento
Time: 1h20min; *Grade:* easy

With your back to the Hotel delle Palme in the centre of Sant'Agata, take the road to the left for 150m/yds, then turn right (this street is identified as Via Termine a little way along). After 50m/yds go left again, down another narrow street (Via Pacliaro di Santolo). Pass beneath the main road, and continue for another 200m/yds. Then ignore a first road on the right but, after another 30m/yds, take the second right (at a T-junction). • This road descends, curves left and levels out. Where it descends sharp right (signed to Sorrento; an alternative route) continue straight ahead on a narrow road, descending gently, then more steeply. When the road ends after 400m/yds, go half-left on a concrete path with a concrete wall on the left. It climbs gently for 150m/yds, to a T-junction, where you turn right down an old paved path. Follow this for about 250m/yds, then continue on a narrow road for another 250m/yds, to an oblique T-junction with a wider road. Turn right downhill for 100m/yds, to the chapel in Crocevia. Turn left down a narrow concrete road which, after 350m/yds, becomes a stepped path passing the chapel of the Madonna della Dolorata. With a Station of the Cross at each bend, you enjoy a spectacular descent to Sorrento. At the bottom, turn left for the old town.

56b Sorrento to Sant'Agata
Time: 1h40min; *Grade:* strenuous, with a *height gain* of 300m/1000ft

From Piazza Tasso in Sorrento take Via San Cesareo (if Signor Tasso's marble lips could move, they would say: 'from here, take the second left'). After 600m/0.35mi, when it ends, cross a road half-left, to ascend an alley (by house number 16) up to the main road. Cross straight over and take a rising side-road. As soon as you can, transfer to the left-hand pavement; this becomes an alley and takes you up to another short stretch of road. At its end, turn right, to climb the steps that zigzag past the Stations of the Cross to the chapel of Madonna della

Dolorata. Soon join a narrow road which leads after 350m/yds to the chapel in Crocevia. • Turn right up the road for 100m/yds, then go sharp left up Via di Schizani. Climbing steadily, after 250m/yds this road becomes a paved path. After a further 250m/yds, in front of a house and garden, turn left onto a concrete path which leads to a narrow road. Climb this steadily for 500m/yds, to where it bends right and widens. Turn left up a narrow road, sign 's AGATA'. This road leads up under a building and the main road, to the town centre. On coming to a T-junction, turn right to the main street.

57 Santa Maria — Marina della Lobra — Massa Lubrense

With its wide views and elegant old buildings along the way, this is an exceptionally fine segment. Only the final ascent to Massa Lubrense disappoints slightly, the paths then being enclosed by walls. **Photograph page 111**

Time: 2h; *Grade:* moderate, with a *height gain* of 120m/390ft

With your back to the church in Santa Maria, go left (Via Annunziata). After 150m/yds, take the narrow road half-right, a short-cut to the next road. Some 100m/yds along this road, look for an alley going right (Salita Castello), up steps to the castle (which always seems to be closed for repairs) and down to the main square in Annunziata with its large church. • Just beyond the square there is a lovely little park with seats and a fine view out to Capri. Continue past the park, descending the road to where it ends by an old house, the Villa Rossi. From here, in 1808, the King of Naples directed the siege of the English who were then occupying Capri, and it was in this house that their surrender was signed, by Hudson Lowe. • Continue down the steps ahead through delightful olive groves, keeping right at a junction of minor roads. On reaching the main road, turn right for 50m/yds, to the church of San Liberatore, which presents fine views down to Marina della Lobra. From the church piazza, take the level path (Via San Liberatore), to contour behind the fishing village for 800m/0.5mi, to a T-junction with a narrow stone- paved road. • From here you should turn left to go down to Marina della Lobra (15min return; bars overlooking the harbour; restaurant open in summer). Retrace your steps and continue uphill to the next junction. Turn left on Via Pipiano. After

100m/yds continue up Via del Canneto; soon steps take you up to a road. Take more steps on the far side and, after 40m/yds, turn left on Via Sirignano. Some 150m/yds along, an old (1728) building faces you; turn right here, up a narrow passage. After 100m/yds turn right up Via Pennino to the main street in Massa Lubrense.

58 Termini — Nerano

This is the first part of a super descent to the clear waters of Ieranto, a World Wild Life conservation area. You could skip this segment by staying on the bus and starting from the next village, Nerano. Having enjoyed a visit to Ieranto (Walk segment 59), you can walk down a delightful path from Nerano to the fleshpots and beach of Marina del Cantone, with an optional extension to Recommone (Walk segment 60).

58a Termini to Nerano

Time: 25min; *Grade:* easy

With your back to the church in Termini, turn left and, after 50m/yds, at the bend, *start* to turn right on Via Campanella. Just under the road name, descend steps. These lead into a path and then a narrow concrete road.
• Follow it downhill for 500m/yds, to a T-junction with another narrow concrete road: turn right. The road narrows to a stepped alley and descends to the road in the centre of Nerano (church, bar and shop).

58b Nerano to Termini

Time: 40min; *Grade:* moderate, with a *height gain* of 170m/560ft

Opposite the church in Nerano, climb the steps (Via Fontana di Nerano). After 100m/yds, turn left up steps through an arch under a house (Via Grottone). After another 300m/ yds (after the path has widened into a minor road), turn left up a narrower concrete road. After a further 500m/yds uphill you reach Termini.

59 Nerano — Ieranto

This 'out and back' walk takes you down to the unspoilt rocky peninsula and delightful small bathing beach of Ieranto, with splendid views along the coast and to Capri. The waters are a World Wild Life site on account of their clarity and abundance of sea life. The timing makes a one hour allowance for exploring, picnicking and bathing — you could easily justify more. Although the track is excellent, the final part and the terrain on the peninsula is rough and rocky — possibly best done in boots. Time: 3h round trip; *Grade:* moderate, with a *height gain* of 170m/560ft

With your back to the church in Nerano, turn left along the road (Via Amerigo Vespucci) for 50m/yds. Take the path leading off right (Via Ieranto). • Continue straight ahead along the track; it ascends gradually for about 1km/0.6mi, contours a steep slope high above the sea, and passes a house (Villa Rosa). (Ignore old signs saying the path is closed because of a landslip.) Then the track narrows and descends for 300m/yds between low walls, to another house on the left. Just beyond this the full view of the peninsula opens out. • Here the path splits; either go right, down a long flight of broken concrete steps to the bathing beach, or fork left and descend to a path between fences that leads to the peninsula and the Saracen tower. • Allow an hour for the return to Nerano.

60 Nerano — Marina del Cantone — Recommone

A delightful, easy path leads from Nerano down past small houses and gardens with snatches of fine views as you go. From Marina del Cantone an easy coastal path takes you round the headland to Recommone, where there is a restaurant and bar (open only in summer). There are beaches at both places, the one at Marina del Cantone being especially well sited. The bars and restaurants in Marina del Cantone are open all year round; the citizens of Sorrento come here to eat in the summer, when their own town is crowded out with visitors. Look for the church of San Antonio at the left-hand end of the beach. **Photograph below**

60a Nerano to Marina del Cantone
Time: 25min plus 30min round trip to Recommone; *Grade:* easy
From Nerano take the passage down to the right of the church (Via Cantone). Follow this all the way down to Marina del Cantone (you cross the main road twice). The path round the headland to Recommone starts at the left-hand side of the beach, to the left of the last restaurant.

60b Marina del Cantone to Nerano
Time: 40min; *Grade:* moderate, with a *height gain* of 150m/500ft
From Marina del Cantone, go up the left-hand side of the large narrow car park (Largo Argentina). This path leads up to the church in Nerano, twice crossing the main road.

Returning from Recommone to Marina del Cantone (Walk segment 60).

61 Termini — Punta Campanella

From Termini an excellent, well-graded track leads down to the lighthouse that marks the extreme tip of the Sorrento Peninsula. On the way you have fine views of Capri, just a few kilometres out to sea.

Time: 2h30min round trip; *Grade:* moderate, with a *height gain* of 320m/1050ft

With your back to the church in Termini, turn left; after 50m/yds, at the bend, turn right down Via Campanella. After 150m/yds, follow the road to the right. This road descends gradually all the way to the lighthouse, with the hillside up to your left. Return the same way.

62 Termini — Monte San Costanzo

The hill topped by the chapel of San Costanzo dominates Termini and can be seen from much of the peninsula, hardly surprising therefore it offers a stupendous panorama, taking in the mountainous spine of the Lattari mountains and both the bays of Naples and Salerno. If you walk to the other of the twin peaks to the west, you have just as good a view of Capri. The peaks are easily reached from Termini by an old track. **Photograph below**

Time: 1h15min (round trip) *Grade:* moderate, with a *height gain* of 160m/500ft

With your back to the church in Termini, turn left; after 50m/yds, at the bend, turn right down Via Campanella. After 150m/yds, at a junction, go straight ahead on Via del Monte. After 150m/yds more, where the road bends right, transfer to the stepped path on the left. This changes to a narrow road and leads up to the road again. The old paved track starts across the road and leads up to the saddle above. Go left to the peak

Climbing up to Monte San Costanzo, with its hilltop chapel (Tour 1 and Walk segment 62).

with the chapel, or go right to follow the road up to the gates of a communications enclosure for the view of Capri. Return the same way. [Confident, well-shod hillwalkers can reach Punta Campanella by a very rough path. From the western end of the saddle, take a narrow path that contours the wooded, then grassy, southern slope of the hill topped by the communications enclosure, to join a well-marked path that descends the southwestern spur. Allow 1h30min.]

63 Colli di San Pietro — Colli di Fontanelle

Colli di San Pietro is the name of the bus stop at the highest point on the Sorrento/Positano road. From here you can easily take this segment to the village of Colli di Fontanelle, then choose between a fine coastal walk to Sant'Agata (Walk segment 65), or the return on foot down to Sorrento (Walk segment 64). (Note that if you are coming from Sorrento, you can take the Circumvesuviana bus from Piano di Sorrento to Colli di Fontanelle.)

63a Colli di San Pietro to Colli di Fontanelle
Time: 35min; *Grade:* easy, with a *height gain* of 70m/230ft

At the Colli di San Pietro, with your back to the gate posts with the name 'Belvedere Massa', walk left along the road towards Sant'Agata for 600m/0.35mi, to a sharp bend to the left. Here take the minor road (Via Bosco) straight ahead; it narrows into a path, crosses a small hill and, after 700m/0.4mi, comes to a T-junction: turn left. Cross the road to ascend a cobbled street, passing a large church on the left. You meet the main road again after 500m/yds, at a crossroads by a bar and shop. This is Colli di Fontanelle.

63b Colli di Fontanelle to Colli di San Pietro
Time: 35min; *Grade:* easy, with a *height gain* of 40m/130ft

From the shop at the crossroads in Colli di Fontanelle, turn left on the main road; 50m/yds along, fork right on a minor street. After 500m/yds you pass a large church on the right and rejoin the main road. Cross straight over, then immediately turn right on a path. It takes you over a small hill, and you regain the road after 700m/0.4mi. Continue ahead on this road for 600m/0.35mi, to meet the Sorrento/Positano road at a crossroads, the Colli di San Pietro.

64 Colli di Fontanelle — Sorrento

The hillsides behind Sorrento have seen quite a lot of new house building, but it is still possible to follow old tracks. On the heights you enjoy expansive views of the Bay of Naples and Sorrento's setting; lower down you wend your way through the interesting older outskirts of the town.

Walk segment 65: the path from Colli di Fontanelle to Sant'Agata for a time goes high above the coast, with distant views along the peninsula.

64a Colli di Fontanelle to Sorrento

Time: 1h30min; *Grade:* easy, with a *height gain* of 60m/200ft

With your back to The Bar in Colli di Fontanelle, turn left onto a narrow level road that starts by contouring the hillside. Soon fork left on Via La Rocca; it climbs gradually, giving magnificent views to the right. On reaching its highest point, the road bends left to meet a crossroads of narrow roads. Turn right onto an earthen road. Descend this for 300m/yds, to a wiggle where it becomes surfaced. After 800m/ 0.5mi more you come to a T-junction by a barrier. Turn right and follow this road round a curve to the left (viewpoint); 400m/yds further on, just after a pair of gateposts on the road and just before a car park, take the narrow road down to the right. Just round the first bend, turn left, straight down the hillside, on a delightful stone-paved path through an olive grove. Eventually you meet a lower, narrow road (Via Casola) at a T-junction: turn left. • Follow this road past Sorrento cemetery; after 600m/0.35mi, at a T-junction with a main road, turn right. Go round the bend, then turn left on a cobbled road. This road comes out on the Via degli Aranci, opposite a road down to Sorrento railway station.

64b Sorrento to Colli di Fontanelle

Time: 1h50min; *Grade:* strenuous, with a *height gain* of 330m/ 1100ft

Facing Sorrento railway station, take the road to the right and follow it up to the main road. Cross directly into Via Marziale. Follow this as it narrows between high walls, to another main road. Turn right, go round the bend for 200m/yds, and turn left into Via S Valerio. Follow this for 800m/0.5mi, past the cemetery, then curving left, to its highest point among houses. Turn right up steps which lead through an olive grove, to a higher wide road by a parking place. • Turn left and take the road up to a right-hand bend. Once round this, turn left past a barrier, up a narrower road. Climb this, often steeply, for 800m/0.5mi, to where it becomes earthen. After a further 300m/yds, at a crossroads of narrow roads, turn left onto a narrow road that descends gradually to Colli di Fontanelle.

65 Colli di Fontanelle — Sant'Agata

The path along the coastline west of Colli di Fontanelle takes a route high above the cliffs to give fantastic views, particularly from a high promontory named Malacoccola reached mid-walk, as far as Capri and back to the highest of the Lattari mountains. Getting nearer to Sant'Agata, the route becomes increasingly domesticated and ends by following minor paths and roads by gardens up to the town centre. The route is equally fine in the other direction. Apart from a short stretch from Sant'Agata, red/white CAI marks will guide you. The hillside on the Sant'Agata side of the Malacoccola viewpoint is steep and rugged, requiring a little easy scrambling. **Photograph opposite**

65a Colli di Fontanelle to Sant'Agata

Time: 2h15min; *Grade:* moderate, with a *height gain* of 250m/800ft

From Colli di Fontanelle climb the minor road (Via Pietrapiana) between the bar and the shop. Go beyond houses, keeping straight ahead, to the main road. Cross it and take a path on the far side, to rejoin the main road higher up. Go left for 200m/yds, to a sharp right-hand bend. Here take the path that ascends gently and then contours towards the coast, through light woodland. Ignore a first turn up right after 70m/yds but, after 100m/yds more, take the second — a narrow well-trodden path that starts by a small isolated hawthorn tree. The path climbs gently and shortly acquires CAI waymarks. It levels out high above the coast. After contouring for 300m/yds, you reach a grassy promontory which provides a grandstand view of the coast, a superb picnic spot.• Now follow CAI marks for 50m/yds (towards a lone island) to the top of a shallow gully down to the right. Following the CAI marks and a well-trodden path, descend the steep rugged hillside to the top edge of a wood. The path now goes left towards the sea, then parallel to the sea, then inland through terraces to the left (lower) side of a lone red-tiled house. • Here the path becomes much wider. Follow it for 1.4km/0.9mi, still with the occasional CAI mark, always straight ahead, contouring across a wild hillside and then through terraces to a gravel, then tarmac road. Continue on the road for 800m/0.5mi to the large church in Torca. • Where the (now) wide road turns right by the church, go ahead down the narrow Via Nula for 100m/yds to a

T-junction. Turn right. Follow this road straight ahead round a left-hand bend, to where it continues as an alley for 100m/yds. Beyond this, on a narrow road again, go 250m/yds to a fork; keep right for 150m/yds more to a left bend. Here turn right up a stepped alley (Il Traversa Pigna) for 300m/yds, up to a minor road. Turn right, then left on the main road to the centre of Sant'Agata.

65b Sant'Agata — Colli di Fontanelle

Time: 2h15min *Grade:* moderate, with a *height gain* of 200m/650ft

With the Hotel delle Palme to your right, go along the main road, past a junction and for 200m/yds more, to where the road bends left. Descend the narrow road straight ahead for 50m/yds, then turn left down an alley (Il Traversa Pigna) for 300m/yds, to a minor road. Turn left and, after 50m/yds, at a fork, keep left on Via Nula. Continue ahead for 400m/yds, until it narrows to an alley. Along here you will pick up the red/white CAI marks which are to be followed for the rest of the walk. Continue ahead and, after 150m/yds (once more on a narrow road), turn left up another narrow road to the large church in Torca. • Go straight ahead and follow the narrow road for 800m/0.5mi through the village of Monticello, until it becomes a gravel road. Continue straight ahead; shortly the way becomes a path which you follow, contouring for 1.4km/0.9mi through terraces and then wild open hillside, until you reach a lone red-tiled house. • Now follow the CAI marks through terracing to the right of the house, climbing gently to the edge of the coast to join a narrow well-trodden path. After 100m/yds this turns inland and ascends the steep rugged hillside ahead. To do this, the CAI marks take you half-left above the wood and then directly up the hillside, zigzagging from time to time, until you reach a grassy promontory which provides a grandstand view of the coast, a superb picnic spot. • Follow the CAI marks parallel with the coast for 300m/yds. The path then descends half-left and finally reaches a level track. Turn left to the main road and turn right along it. After 200m/yds, turn right down Via Pietrapiana to the main road again. Cross it and follow the minor road down to Colli di Fontanelle (shop, bar).

❀ Capri

Capri lies six kilometres out to sea, an elongated rocky protuberance 7km long and 3km across at its widest point. It is ringed by high limestone cliffs much of the way round, rising to 589m/1900ft at its highest point, Monte Solaro. Above the cliffs the terrain, although hilly, is gentle enough to allow habitation and gardening on the fertile soil. The main town of Capri occupies the spine of the eastern half of the island, spilling down the slopes north and south to the harbours of Marina Grande and Marina Piccola. A cliff crosses the island, isolating the western half, occupied by the higher town of Anacapri (a much quieter place than its brasher neighbour). A road has been cut into the cliff-face to connect the two towns, and a funicular railway will whisk you up from the Marina Grande to Capri town.

In summer an endless stream of large modern ferries disgorges so many day visitors onto the Marina Grande that congestion hinders people getting to the funicular and, when they do finally succeed, they fill to over-flowing the squares of the main town up on its hilltop. Then, while browsing in the boutiques, they complain of the crush. But here, as anywhere else, you can get away from the crowds in no time at all ... and walk through the tranquil flower-bedecked world that has enticed so many of the rich and famous to live here. Narrow roads swathed in bougainvillaea and redolent of jasmine, and used only by pedestrians and the occasional electric

The Villa Malaparte, a futuristic house lying low on a headland, built for writer Curzio Malaparte in 1938 by the Trentino architect Libera (Walk segment 68).

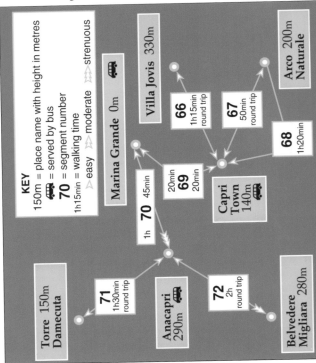

KEY
150m = place name with height in metres
 = served by bus
70 = segment number
1h15min = walking time
△ = easy △△ = moderate △△△ = strenuous

trolley, lead past fine houses with ornamental and kitchen gardens to the island's sensational coastline. A visit to this magical place should figure in every itinerary, and best of all in winter.

Getting about

The *funicular* will take you efficiently in just a few minutes from the Marina Grande up to the main town. *Buses* go from both the Marina Grande and Capri town along the switchback road to Anacapri, higher up to the west and, from there, a bus runs down to the Blue Grotto (Grotta Azzura). From Anacapri you can take the *chair lift* to the summit of Monte Solaro (Excursion 17; photograph page 23). Tip for jumping the queue for the bus from Anacapri to Capri or Marina Grande: walk 300m/yds on the road away from Capri to the next (earlier) bus stop.

Tourist sights

Apart from Villa Jovis (see Walk segment 66), in Capri

you could visit the restored monastery of Certosa, or the Gardens of Augusto, for their view. In Anacapri there is the Villa San Michele (Walk segment 70), once home to the Swedish writer Axel Munthe, now a museum, built around the remains of a Roman villa.

Walk planning tips

The segments 66, 67 and 68 together offer a full day's walking, at a reasonably gentle pace to allow time for sight-seeing. They effectively cover the eastern end of the island, the most popular part. Views change rapidly and interest is always there. If you wish to do just one or two of these, segments 67 and 68 probably provide more variety than 66. Walk segment 69 takes you easily back down to the harbour at the end of the day.

Walk segment 70 offers a most dramatic alternative to the overcrowded bus for getting to or from Anacapri. Walk segments 71 and 72 are easy strolls on the western half of the island, visiting a finely-sited Roman villa and taking in some spectacular coastal scenery. Both start in Anacapri which is itself delightful to explore.

WALK SEGMENTS

66 Capri — Villa Jovis

This segment takes you up to the superbly-situated Roman villa at the top of the island's easternmost peak; the site itself is well worth the time and cost of entrance. (Entrance is free for EU citizens under 18 or over 60; take your passport as proof.)

Time: 1h15min round trip; *Grade:* easy, with a *height gain* of 200m/ 660ft

From the funicular in Capri, turn left around the main tower, into a little square. Go through the small arch in the far left-hand side, on Via Longano (you could buy your picnic here). After 100m/yds bend right, into Via Sopramonte. Follow this for 400m/yds, to a crossroads, where the Villa Jovis is signposted to the left and the Arco Naturale straight on. Go left. • This path climbs gently but steadily for 1.5km/1mi to the Villa Jovis (•• on the left after 40m/yds and another at public toilets half-way along; restaurant/bar two-thirds of the way up). Return same way to the crossroads.

67 Capri — Arco Naturale

This large natural arch is set in a fine piece of pine-clad cliff scenery, with an azure sea far below. The path takes you there easily. There are some seats there for your picnic, or a well-situated bar/restaurant on the path five minutes before the arch. **Photograph overleaf**

Time: 50min round trip; *Grade:* easy, with a *height gain* of 100m/330ft

Follow **Walk segment 66** (page 123) to the crossroads, then go straight ahead (Via Matermania; signposted 'Arco Naturale'). Return the same way or by Walk segment 68.

68 Arco Naturale to Capri via the coast path

A very well built path takes you around the rugged southeastern cliffs, with an easy return to town along a delightfully verdant alley. On the way you

Looking through the Arco Naturale to the coast far below (Excursion 16, Walk segment 67)

encounter various points of interest — the Grotta di Matermania, a large cave with Roman remains; the Villa Malaparte (see page 121); and the famous Faraglione islands (photograph page 23), three limestone fangs rising from a blue sea — Capri's iconic feature when viewed from along the Amalfi Coast. **Photograph page 121**

Time: 1h20min; *Grade:* easy, with a *height gain* of 50m/160ft

From the restaurant near the Arco Naturale, descend the long flight of steep steps signposted 'Grotta Matermania'. This path levels out at the cave and then leads you easily by the landmarks mentioned above. Finally, on reaching the narrow town road (Via Tragara), go ahead for 800m/0.5mi, to a crossroads by a small square (Li Campi). Go right for 100m/yds, past boutiques, to the main square.

69 Marina Grande — Capri town

It's pretty simple to go either way on foot.

69a Marina Grande to Capri town

Time: 20 min; *Grade:* easy, with a *height gain* of 140m/460ft

Facing the funicular station, go left on the quay for 100m/yds, to a small square. Turn right up a road and, after 50m/yds, go left up Via Truglio. Steps give way to paving and lead you, always up and ahead at junctions, to the centre of Capri town.

69a Capri town to Marina Grande

Time: 20 min; *Grade:* easy

Take steps down by the clock tower and funicular station. Turn left on Via Acquaviva. Follow this downhill until you can see a road about 50m/yds ahead. Turn right immediately and cross the road into Via Truglio, which leads down to the harbour.

70 Marina Grande — Anacapri

The Phoenician Steps (Scala Fenicia) were built in the middle ages to connect Anacapri with the outside world via the harbour at Marina Grande and force a breach in the formidable cliff that divides the island of Capri in two. Nearly all commerce, people and goods, had to go up or down this switchback flight of steps. In 1877 the road was built allowing wheeled traffic, and the steps consequently fell out of use and crumbled. In 1999, the authorities, realising their historical importance and tourist potential, repaired them and re-opened them for pedestrians — and a very good job they have done. Despite their dramatic position, walkers need feel no sense of vertigo as the balustrade is always substantial. But there is no getting away from the height to be climbed, so the 995 steps from harbour to top will always be a tough slog. **Photograph pages 126-127**

70a Marina Grande — Anacapri

Time: 1h; *Grade:* strenuous, with a *height gain* of 290m/950ft

With your back to the sea, take the motor road going up right from the harbour for 250m/yds, to the first pedestrian crossing. Turn left up steps to the road again and go down right along it for 100m/yds, to find an alley on the left. Turn up this (Scala Fenicia). Now just continue straight ahead, ever more steeply up to the zigzags up the cliff. Continue to pass under the road and a final flight of steps up to the Villa San Michele. Take the boutique-lined alley from here for 400m/yds to Piazza Vittoria.

70b Anacapri — Marina Grande
Time: 45min; *Grade:* easy, with a *descent* of 290m/950ft

From Piazza Vittoria take the broad steps up towards the cable car station, and turn left onto the alley to Villa San Michele. The steps start beyond the villa. Soon go under the cliff road. After the zigzags, the descent is less steep. On meeting a road, turn right for 100m/yds, then turn left down more steps to the road again. Turn right for the harbour.

71 Anacapri — Torre Damecuta

This 'out and back' route takes you through the delightful town of Anacapri, amongst its outlying houses and gardens, and finally to a super viewpoint with a medieval tower and extensive Roman remains. Return by the same route or pick up one of the buses returning from the Grotta Azzurra. **Photograph pages 4-5**

Time: 1h30min round trip; *Grade:* easy, with a *height gain* of 140m/460ft (on the return)

From the Piazza Vittoria in Anacapri (the second bus stop on reaching the town), take the path that descends

gently between shops. After 200m/yds pass the Casa Rossa on the right (note the ornate doorway). In a further 100m/yds turn right on Via San Nicola (where a map of the western half of the island is depicted in ceramic tiles). Go past the church of San Michele on the left (which has an exceptionally beautiful ceramic floor),beyond which the path bends left into a narrow passage. You pass to the left of the residence of a former parliamentary deputy, Giuseppe Orlandi, responsible for the construction of the motor road to Anacapri in 1877. • The passage joins a wider alley, with bougainvillaea-clad palms in its centre. This bends to the right. Soon fork right, then turn left at a T-junction, to join a minor motor road. At this point the roads are named, and you walk from Via Boffe to Via la Vigna. After 150m/yds turn left into Traversa la Vigna. This descends gradually, becomes wider and opens up views of Ischia on the skyline. After 350m/yds on the *traversa,* where the path bends to the right, descend steps straight ahead. • After 500m/yds there are turnings off to the left and right; keep ahead. The way narrows into a path beyond a barrier. After 250m/yds the path ends at a crossroads; turn left on Traversa Damecuta. On reaching a main road after 100m/yds, turn right. This main road turns left immediately: go straight ahead (Via Amadeo Mauri). This leads after 400m/yds along a splendid balcony path, to the Torre Damecuta site.

• If the site is locked, with care you can get over the fence easily, just as the locals do. Inside there are Roman and medieval remains, information boards in English, and pine trees for a shady picnic. To return, go back to the main road and there either pick up a bus coming up from the Blue Grotto (pay on board) or walk back the same way — take the first left, the first right, and then the upward choice at all junctions.

The Phoenician Steps snake up the cliff to Anacapri (Walk segment 70)

72 Anacapri — Belvedere Migliara

This segment visits the southwest of the island, with views to the lighthouse, then follows the coast path up to a spectacular viewpoint looking past towering cliffs to the Faraglione Islands. On the way to the belvedere we go through the little village of Caprile; coming back (by a different route) we follow a minor road with extensive views. (The viewpoint may also be reached directly from the Piazza Vittoria: take Via Caposcuro by the chairlift station; after 400m/yds fork left, then go straight ahead.)

Time: 2h round trip; *Grade;* moderate, with a *height gain* of 190m/620ft

From the Piazza Vittoria in Anacapri, take the path that descends gently between shops. After 400m/yds you come to a T-junction, where the white church of Santa Sofia is on the right. Turn left. Another delightful alley takes you to a minor motor road. Cross and continue ahead on Via Caprile for 200m/yds, to the piazza in Caprile (the terminus for buses coming from Capri).
• Descend the steps (Via Falligara). After 100m/yds, at a fork, keep left downhill. At a T-junction turn left along Via Faro. After 300m/yds, at a junction by a glass-cased Madonna, turn right and then left. In a further 150m/yds you reach a motor road: go right but, after 50m/yds, turn left on a narrow road. You pass the entrance (on your right) to the medieval Torre di Materita, owned by the Munthe family (of the Villa San Michele in Anacapri) and not open to the public. The path skirts the wall (on your right) of the estate, descending, then climbing gradually. After 1km/0.6mi you reach the gate of the Torre Guardia, a medieval fortification reconstructed by the English during their occupation of the island in 1807. • Go left, then immediately right on a narrow footpath (beside the end wall of the *torre* grounds). This path now follows the coast for about 600m/0.35mi, climbing through bushes. The views along the cliffs and back down to the Punta Carena lighthouse are stunning. • You reach a narrow paved road at a viewpoint with seats. But continue by path, up to a more spectacular viewpoint about 100m/yds further up the coast (more seats, and views out to the Faraglione Islands). • To return to Anacapri, go back to the first viewpoint and follow the narrow paved road for 2km/1.2mi to the Piazza Vittoria. The way is level, and you enjoy fine views of the island and across the bay to Ischia as you go. There is a restaurant (open only in summer) not far past the viewpoint.

BUS TIMETABLES

Below are the bus stops shown in the walk planners, followed by the numbers of the relevant *timetables* we list below. All services are operated by the SITA bus company, unless otherwise stated. See information about bus travel on pages 8-9 and price guide on page 133. Sunday- and holiday-only services, and some early and late services have been omitted. *You should confirm these times locally before travelling.*

Amalfi 1, 2, 3, 4, 5, 6
Anacapri 12
Atrani 1, 3
Bomerano 6
Capo 8, 9
Cetara 1
Colli di Fontanelle 11

Colli di San Pietro 2
Conca dei Marini 2
Erchie 2
Furore 2
Grotta Azzurra 12
Maiori 1, 5
Marina del Cantone 9, 10

Marina Grande 12
Massa Lubrense 8, 9
Minori 1
Monte Pertuso 7
Nerano 9, 10
Nocelle 7
Pietre 5
Pogerola 4

Polvica 5
Positano 2, 7
Praiano 2
Ravello 3
Salerno 1
San Lazzaro 6
Sant'Agata 8, 10, 11

Sta Maria de Olearia 1
Scala 3
Sorrento 2, 8, 9, 10
Termini 9, 10
Vèttica Maggiore 2

1 Amalfi — Salerno, via Minori and Maiori

Salerno	Maiori	Minori	Amalfi	Amalfi	Minori	Maiori	Salerno
06.45	07.35	07.40	07.55	06.00	06.15	06.20	07.10
08.00*	08.50*	08.55*	09.10*	06.30*	06.45*	06.50*	07.40*
09.00	09.50	09.55	10.10	07.00*	07.15*	07.20*	08.10*
10.00	10.50	10.55	11.10	07.15*	07.30*	07.35*	08.25*
10.30*	11.20*	11.25*	11.40*	08.05	08.20	08.25	09.15
11.30	12.20	12.25	12.40	09.00*	09.15*	09.20*	10.10*
12.00*	12.50*	12.55*	13.10*	10.00	10.15	10.20	11.10
12.45	13.35	13.40	13.55	11.00	11.15	11.20	12.10
13.30*	14.20*	14.25*	14.40*	12.10	12.25	12.30	13.20
14.10	15.00	15.05	15.20	12.50*	13.05	13.10	14.00
14.30*	15.20*	15.25*	15.40*	13.15*	13.30*	13.35*	14.25*
15.30	16.20	16.25	16.40	14.15	14.30	14.35	15.25
16.30	17.20	17.25	17.40	15.15	15.30	15.35	16.25
17.00*	17.50*	17.55*	18.10*	16.00	16.15	16.20	17.10
17.30	18.20	18.25	18.40	17.00*	17.15*	17.20*	18.10*
18.30*	19.20*	19.25*	19.40*	18.00	18.15	18.20	19.10
19.30	20.20	20.25	20.40	19.00	19.15	19.20	20.10
20.30	21.20	21.25	21.40	20.00*	20.15*	20.20*	20.10*
21.30*	22.20*	22.25*	22.40*	21.00	21.15	21.20	22.10
22.30	23.20	23.25	23.40	22.00*	22.15*	22.20*	23.10*

*not on Sundays or holidays. *Bus stop sequence:* Amalfi, Atrani, Minori, Maiori, Santa Maria de Olearia, Erchie, Cetara, Salerno

2 Sorrento — Amalfi, via Positano and Praiano

Sorrento	Positano	Praiano	Amalfi	Amalfi	Praiano	Positano	Sorrento
06.30*	07.10*	07.35*	08.00*	06.30	06.55	07.10	08.10
08.30	09.10	09.35	10.00	07.15*	07.40*	07.55*	08.55*
08.45*]	09.50*]	10.15*]	10.40*]	08.05	08.30	08.45	09.45
09.15/	10.05/	10.30/	10.55/	09.00*/	09.25*/	09.40*/	10.40*/
09.30*/	10.10*/	10.45*/	11.10*/	09.30/	09.55/	10.10/	11.10/
09.45*/	10.35*/	11.00*/	11.25*/	11.00/	11.25/	11.40/	12.40/
10.05/	10.55/	11.20/	11.45/	11.30/	11.55/	12.10/	13.10/
10.30*	11.20*	11.45*	12.10*	12.15/	12.40/	12.55/	13.55/
11.00*/	11.50*/	12.15*/	12.40*/	13.00*/	13.25*/	13.40*/	14.40*/
11.30/	12.20/	12.45/	13.10/	13.30/	13.55/	14.10/	15.10/
12.30	13.10	13.35	14.00	14.05/	14.30/	14.45/	15.45/
13.00/	13.50/	14.15/	14.40/	14.30	14.55	15.10	16.10
13.30	14.10	14.35	15.00	15.15/	15.40/	15.55/	16.55/
14.15*	14.55*	15.20*	15.45*	16.00	16.25	16.40	17.40
15.30]	16.35]	17.00]	17.25]	16.30	16.55	17.10	18.10
16.00*	16.40*	17.05*	17.30*	17.00*	17.25*	17.40*/	18.40*/
16.30	17.10	17.35	18.00	17.30/	17.55/	18.10/	19.10/
17.00/	17.50/	18.15/	18.40/	18.15*/	18.40*/	19.55*/	19.55*/
17.45*/	18.35*/	19.00*/	19.25*/	19.00]	19.25]	19.40]	20.55]

Timetable 2 continues on the next page

*not on Sundays or holidays;] via Sant'Agata; / via bivio Sant'Agata; see note at foot of page 130. *Bus stop sequence:* Sorrento, Colli di San Pietro, Positano, Vettica Maggiore, Praiano, Furore, Conca, Amalfi

2 Sorrento — Amalfi *(Continued)*

Sorrento	Positano	Praiano	Amalfi	Amalfi	Praiano	Positano	Sorrento
18.25/	19.05/	19.25/	19.55/	19.30*/	19.55*/	20.10*/	20.10*/
19.25/	20.15/	20.40/	21.05/	20.00/	20.25/	20.40/	21.40/
20.00/	20.50/	21.15/	21.40/	21.00/	21.25/	21.40/	22.40/
21.00/	21.50/	22.15/	22.40/	22.00/	22.25/	22.40/	23.40/
22.00/	22.50/	23.15/	23.40/				

*not on Sundays or holidays;] via Sant'Agata; / via bivio Sant'Agata; see note at foot of page 130. *Bus stop sequence:* Sorrento, Colli di San Pietro, Positano, Vettica Maggiore, Praiano, Furore, Conca, Amalfi

3 Amalfi — Ravello — Amalfi, via Scala

The following departures leave: both Ravello and Scala, the sequence varying; Ravello only (R); or Scala only (S). Journey time approximately 30min

Departures from Amalfi: 6.30*, 7.05*S, 8.00, 9.00, 9.15*R, 10.00, 10.15*R, 11.00, 11.15*R, 12.10*, 12.15*, 12.45*R, 13.30*, 14.00*, 14.30*, 15.00*, 15.35, 16.00*, 16.35, 17.00*, 17.30*, 18.15*, 18.50, 19.00*, 19.30*R, 20.00, 21.30*,22.00, 23.00, 0.00, 1.00

Departures from Ravello and/or Scala: 5.40*, 6.00*, 6.30*, 7.30*R, 7.35*, 8.35*(S), 9.25, 1030*, 10.45*R, 1125, 11.40*, 12.45*, 13.15*R, 13.55*, 14.25*, 14.55*, 15.30*R, 16.10R, 16.10*, 16.25*, 17.00*, 17.25*, 18.10*S, 18.50*, 19.35R, 19.35*, 20.00*R, 20.40*S, 21.30*, 22.25, 23.25, 0.25*

*not on Sundays or holidays

4 Amalfi — Pogerola — Amalfi

Journey time 20min each way

Departures from Amalfi: 7.20*, 8.10, 9.00, 10.00, 11.00, 11.40, 12.00*, 12.20, 13.20, 14.20*, 15.10*, 15.30**, 16.00*, 16.50, 17.30*, 18.10, 19.00, 19.20**, 19.30*, 20.00*, 20.15**, 21.05, 22.00, 22.40, 23.45*

Departures from Pogerola: 5.30, 5.55*, 6.40*, 7.40, 8.40, 9.40, 10.40, 11.20*, 12.00, 12.30*, 12.45**, 13.00, 14.45*, 15.30*, 16.00**, 16.30, 17.20, 17.50*, 18.40, 19.40, 20.40, 21.25, 22.20

*not on Sundays or holidays; **Sundays and holidays only; journey time 20min.

5 Maiori — Polvica — Pietre (for Tramonti)

Maiori	Polvica	Pietre	Pietre	Polvica	Maiori
06.55*	07.15*	07.25*			
08.20*	08.40*	08.50*			
09.20*§	09.40*/	10.00*			
10.20*	10.40*/	11.00*	10.35*	10.55*/	11.15*
11.25*	11.45*/	12.05*	13.10*	13.20*	13.40*
12.30*§	12.50*	13.00*	14.30*	14.40*	15.00*
13.35*§	13.55*/	14.15*	17.00*	17.10*	17.30*
15.20*	15.40*	15.50*	17.55*	18.05*	18.25*
17.30*	17.50*/	18.10*			

*not on Sundays or holidays
/detours to Corsano and returns to Polvica
§terminates at Amalfi; 20min earlier or later
Note: leaves Maiori from near Bar Oriente

Note on Sorrento — Amalfi routes: Between Sorrento and Colli di San Pietro the bus usually goes via Sant'Agnello and Meta; if marked / against the times in the table, it takes the 'Nastro Verde' road west and south out of Sorrento with a stop at Bivio Sant'Agata, the main road junction 500m/yds east of Sant'Agata town centre; times marked] have stops at Massa Lubrense and Sant'Agata centre. These routes allow people in Sant'Agata to get easily to the Amalfi coast, and vice versa, overcrowding permitting.

6 Amalfi — Bomerano — San Lazzaro (for Agerola)

Amalfi	Bomerano	San Lazzaro	San Lazzaro	Bomerano	Amalfi
07.10*	07.50*	08.05*	09.45*	10.00*	10.40*
08.05*	08.45*	09.00*	12.10*	12.258	13.05*
10.15	10.55	11.10	13.10*	13.25*	14.05*
11.40*	12.20*	12.35*	15.00	15.15	15.55
13.20*	14.00*	14.15*	16.05*	16.20*	17.00*
14.15*	14.55*	15.10*	16.30*	16.45*	17.25*
15.30	16.10	16.25	17.00*	17.15*	17.55*
17.00	17.40	17.55	18.00	18.15	18.55
18.15*	18.55*	19.10*	19.20	19.35	20.15
19.00	19.40	19.55			
20.50*	21.20*	21.45*			

*not on Sundays or holidays

7 Positano — Monte Pertuso — Nocelle — Positano

Positano	Nocelle	Positano
08.00	08.20	08.40
10.20	10.40	11.00
12.20	12.40	13.00
14.20	14.40	15.00
17.20	17.40	18.00
19.20	19.40	20.00

Notes

1 This service is operated by Positano town buses; purchase tickets on board.

2 Monte Pertuso lies on the road to Nocelle.

3 If travelling by bus along the coast road, connect with this service at 'Bivio Monte Pertuso' — where the mountain road leaves the coast road. This bus arrives here about 10min after departure from Positano centre (Piazza dei Mulini).

8 Sorrento — Massa Lubrense — Sant'Agata

Sorrento	Massa Lubrense	Sant' Agata	Sant' Agata	Massa Lubrense	Sorrento
07.25	07.45	08.00	06.15	06.30	06.50
08.05	08.25	08.40	07.10	07.25	07.45
08.50	09.10	09.25	07.45	08.00	08.20
09.30*	09.50*	10.05*	08.30	08.45	09.05
10.10	10.30	10.45	09.15	09.30	09.50
11.00	11.20	11.35	10.20	10.35	10.55
12.15	12.35	12.50	11.15	11.30	11.50
13.00*	13.20*	13.35*	12.10	12.25	12.45
13.15	13.35	13.50	12.50	13.05	13.25
14.00	14.20	14.35	13.15	13.30	13.50
15.25*	15.45*	16.00*	14.20	14.35	13.55
16.15	16.35	16.50	15.25	15.40	16.00
17.10*	17.30*	17.45*	16.00	16.15	16.35
18.00*	18.20*	18.35*	17.00*	17.15*	17.35*
19.15	19.35	19.40	17.10	17.25	17.45
20.05	20.25	20.40	18.00*	18.15*	18.35*
21.05	21.25	21.40	19.05	19.20	19.40
22.10	22.30	22.45	20.20	20.35	20.55
23.00	23.20	23.35	21.30	21.45	22.05
			22.20*	22.35*	22.55*

*not on Sundays or holidays
Note: Capo lies between Sorrento and Massa Lubrense.

9 Sorrento — Massa Lubrense — Marina del Cantone

Sorrento	Massa Lubrense	Termini	Marina del Cantone	Marina del Cantone	Termini	Massa Lubrense	Sorrento
07.50	08.10	08.30	08.45	06.55	07.10	07.25	07.45
11.30*	11.50*	12.05*	12.20*	09.00	09.15	09.35	09.55
13.35	13.55	14.15	14.30	16.00*	16.15*	16.45*	17.05*
14.50*	15.10*	15.30*	15.45*	19.00	19.15	19.35	19.55
18.00*	18.20*	18.40*	18.55*				
20.05	20.25	20.45	21.00				

*not on Sundays or holidays
Note: Nerano lies between Termini and Marina del Cantone; Capo lies between Sorrento and Massa Lubrense

10 Sorrento — Sant'Agata — Marina del Cantone

Sorrento	Sant' Agata	Termini	Marina del Cantone	Marina del Cantone	Termini	Sant' Agata	Sorrento
06.50*	07.15*					09.00*	06.25*
08.05*	08.30*					07.00	07.25
08.50	09.15	09.35	09.50			07.25*	07.50*
10.10	10.35	10.55	11.10			08.15	08.40
12.15	12.40					08.30*	08.55*
13.15	13.40					08.45	09.10
14.00	14.25	14.45	15.00			09.00*	09.25*
15.30	15.55	16.15	16.30	10.20	10.35	10.55	11.20
16.15	16.40	17.00	17.10	11.30	11.45	12.10	12.35
18.00	18.25					13.00	13.25
19.15	19.40			12.35*	12.50*	13.10*	
21.05	21.30	21.50		14.30	14.45	15.05	15.30
22.00*	22.45*			15.00	15.15	15.35	16.00
23.00*	23.45*			16.30	16.45	17.05	17.30
23.40	00.05			17.30	17.45	17.55	
						18.00	18.25
						19.30	19.55
						20.40	21.05
				21.00	21.15	21.25	
					21.50	22.10	

*not on Sundays or holidays
Notes
1   Nerano lies between Termini and Marina del Cantone.
2   Between Sorrento and Sant'Agata the bus takes the Nastro Verde road.

11 Piano di Sorrento — Fontanelle — Sant'Agata

Piano	Colli di Fontanelle	Sant'Agata	Sant'Agata	Colli di Fontanelle	Piano
06.50	07.10	07.20	07.20	07.30	07.50
08.20	08.40	08.50	08.50	09.00	09.20
09.50	10.10	10.20	10.20	10.30	10.50
11.20	11.40	11.50	11.50	12.00	12.20
12.50	13.10	13.20	13.20	13.30	13.50
14.20	14.40	14.50	14.50	15.00	15.20
15.50	16.10	16.20	16.20	16.30	16.50
17.20	17.40	17.50	17.50	18.00	18.20
18.50	19.10	19.20	19.20	19.30	19.50
			21.20	21.30	21.50

*not on Sundays or holidays. *Note:* This service is operated by Circumvesuviana, leaving from a road by Piano di Sorrento Station.

12 Services on Capri

The service on the island is operated by Capri Buses. Purchase tickets on board (€1.30), except on leaving Capri town, where there is a ticket office. Buses are relatively frequent. Routes: Marina Grande — Capri
Marina Grande — Anacapri
Capri — Anacapri
Anacapri — Grotta Azzurra

13 Sorrento town buses

The yellow town buses run a frequent service on four routes:
Linea A: Capo — Piazza Tasso — S Agnello — Piano — Meta
Linea B: Marina Piccola — Piazza Tasso — station
Linea C: Marina Piccola — Piazza Tasso — S Agnello
Shuttle service: Marina Piccola — Piazza Tasso

14 Naples airport — Salerno

Coaches currently leave the airport for Salerno at: 10.30, 14.45, 18.30, 21.30. They leave Salerno for the airport at: 07.00, 13.00, 16.00, 19.00.

Notes: Journey time about one hour. Tickets (€7.00) purchased on board. Salerno stop in Piazza Tasso at bus terminus.

15 Naples airport — Sorrento

Coaches currently leave the airport for Sorrento at: 09.00, 11.30, 13.00, 14.30, 16.30, 19.30. They leave Sorrento for the airport at: 06.30, 08.30, 10.30, 12.00, 14.00, 16.30.

Notes: Journey time about one hour. Tickets (€7.00) purchased on board. Sorrento stop in Piazza Tasso.

Bus tickets and prices

Except for the Positano town bus and travel on Capri, a **unified ticket system** operates — 'Unico Campania'. These tickets are valid on SITA, Circumvesuviana and Sorrento buses, and must be bought in tobacconists *(tabacchi)* or bars before boarding. On buses the tickets allow a specified number of minutes' travel, including changes, at a number of time/fare levels: up to 45 minutes €2.00; up to 90 minutes €3.00; 24 hours €6.00; 3 days €15.00.

The AST (tourist office) in Sorrento has photocopies of the current timetables 2, 8, 9, 10, 11 and 13; also for ferries to Capri and the cable car from Castellamare to Mont Faito. The Amalfi SITA?ticket office has a sheet with timetables 1, 2, 3, and 4.

Useful Web Sites

The official Sorrento tourist site (www.sorrentotourism.com) is a mine of information, including details of accomodation and travel. It has full ferry timetables for services in the Bay of Naples and to Capri.

The sites for Positano, Amalfi and Ravello are as follows: www.aziendaturismopositano.it, www.amalfitouristoffice.it and www.ravellotime.it.

SITA bus timetables can be seen on www.sitabus.it. First click on *linie regionali, Campania, orari,* then you need *quadro* VII (Amalfi/Tramonti plus a daily Naples service), XIII (Amalfi/Agerola and Naples), XIV (Sorrento/Sant'Agata/Massa Lubrense/Marina del Cantone and Sorrento/Amalfi), XV-A1 and XV-A2 (Sorrento/Amalfi and Amalfi local services).

Sorrento trains and other bus services: www.vesuviana.it.

For ferries (apart from those in the Bay of Naples) go to www.metrodelmare.com for the Sorrento/Positano/Amalfi/Salerno service. Other Amalfi coast ferry services can be seen on www.amalficoastweb.com.

Index

This index contains geographical names only. For other entries, see Contents, page 3. Page numbers in **bold** indicate a photograph; those in *italic* a town plan or an entry in a walk planner. Pronunciation guide: where a syllable in a place name is in **bold,** stress that syllable. Otherwise stress the next to last syllable (eg. **Amal**fi).

Agerola 7, 21, 30, 38, 60
Amalfi 7, 9, 10, 19, 20, **24-25**, **34-35**, 36, 38, *39*, 40, 43, **44**, 45, 50, 51, **81**, 82, 87
 Town plan *36*
Anacapri 23, 121, *122*, 123, 125, **126-127**, 128
Annu**n**ziata 26, 113
Arco Naturale 23, *122*, **124**
Atrani **8**, **12-13**, 20, **21**, 25, 34, 37, *39,* **40-42**, 54, **55**, **56**

Belvedere Migliara *122*, 128
Bomerano 30, 38, 60, *61*, 73, 78, 79
Bosco Grande 45, 53

Campi**d**oglio *39,* 47
Capo 23
Capri **4-5**, 7, **9**, 19, **23**, **26-27**, 103, **121**, *122*, 123-128
Caserma Forestale *61*, **65**, 66
Cetara 89, 97
Colle la Serra *61*, **70-74**
Colli di Fontanelle 27, *102*, 103, 117, **118**, 119
Colli di San Pietro 58, *61,* 75, 100, *102*, 117
Conca dei Marini 7, 10, 22, 25, 38, **81**, *82*, 84-86

Erchie *89*, 97
Ercolano (Hercu**lan**eum) 10, 30

Ieranto *102*, 114
I **Tra**siti 65, **67**

Lone *39*, 49

Maiori 7, 10, **14**, 22, 25, 33, 88, *89*, 91-95, **98**
Marina della Lobra *102*, 113

Marina del Cantone 23, 27, *102*, **115**
Marina di Furore 58, *61*, **75**, 79
Marina di Puolo *102*, 104
Marina Grande 121, *122*, 125
Massa Lubrense 19, 26, 100, *102*, 103, 105, 106, 109, 110, 113
Minori 7, 10, 22, 25, 34, *39*, 44, 54, 57, 88, *89*, 90, 93, **98**
Minuta *39*, 45-48, 52
Monte Comune **65**, **67**, 76-77
Monte Faito 23, 28
Monte Pertuso 22, 29, **32**, 58, 60, *61*, 62, 63, 64, 65
Monte Solaro **23**, 122

Napoli (Naples) 4, 9, 10, 31
Nerano 23, *102*, 103, 114, 115
Nocelle 22, 29, 58, *61*, 63, 64, 70

Paestum 30, **31**
Pantano **12**, *102*, 103, **104**, 105
Pastena *39*, 49
Pianillo 30
Pietre 89, 95
Po**ger**ola 20, 32, 34, *39*, 43, 50, 52, *82*
Polvica 88, *89*, 93
Pompei 4, 10, 30
Pontepri**mari**o 96
Pontone 32, *39*, 45, 47, 51, 54, 56
Positano 7, 9, 10, 22, 23, **28-29**, 38, 58, 59, 60, *61*, 62, 63, 67, **68-69, cover**
 Town plan *59*
Positano (Bar Internazionale) 58, *61*, 67-69

Praiano 7, 10, 25, 58, 60, *61,* 71, 78, 79
Pucara *89,* 96
Punta Campanella *102,* 116
Ravello **1,** 7, **8,** 10, **12-13,** 19, 20, 22, **31,** 34, 36, 37, *39,* 41, **42-43,** 44, 46, 47, 57, *89,* 93
   Town plan *37*
Recommone *102,* **115**

Salerno 9, 10, 25, 30
Sambuco 88, *89,* 93
San Costanzo 26, 100, *102,* **116**
San Domenico **2,** *61,* **71,** 74
San Lazzaro 21, 31, 38, *39, 82,* **83,** 84
San Nicola *89,* 93
Santa Caterina 47
Sant'Agata 19, 27, 100, *102,* 103, 107, 110, 112, **118,** 119
Santa Maria 26, *102,* 108, 109, 113
Santa Maria del Castello **28-29,** *61,* 66, 67, **68-69,** 75
Santa Maria de Olearia 88, *89,* 91, **92**
Santuario dell'Avvocata 88, *89,* **97,** 98

Scala 19, *39,* 46
Sorrento 4, 7, 10, 19, 23, 26, 100, *101, 102,* 103, 104, 106, 112, 117
   Town plan *101*
Spiaggia di Conca dei Marini *22*

Termini **9,** 23, **26-27,** *102,* 103, 107, 108, 114, 116
Torello *39,* 44, 54, 55
Torre Damecuta **5,** *122,* 126
Torre dello Ziro 38, *39,* **44,** 46, **56**
Tovere *82,* 84-87
Tramonti 7, **32-33,** 88, 93, **94,** 95, **136**
Trugnano *89,* 96

Valle dei Mulini (Valley of the Mills) *39,* 51
Valle delle Ferriere *39,* 52, **53**
Vesuvio (Vesuvius) 4, 30, **104**
Vèttica Maggiore 24, 58, 60, *61,* 71, **72-73,** 74, 78, 79
Vèttica Minore 87
Villa Cimbrone **1, 8,** 20, 22, 37, 41, 43
Villa Jovis 23, *122,* 123
Villa di **Poll**io 23, *102,* 104

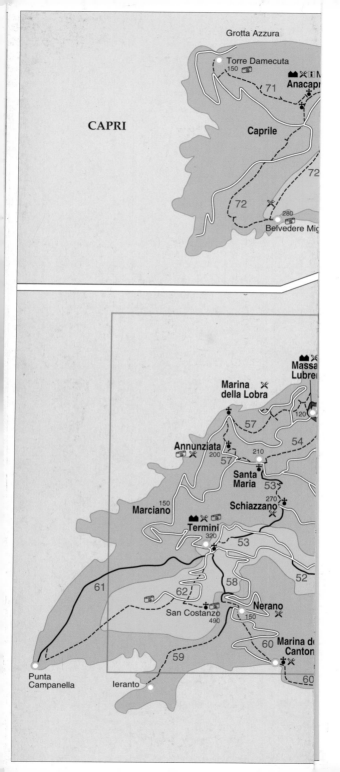